PRACTICAL SOLUTIONS TO YOUR GREATEST MANAGEMENT CHALLENGES

LEADERSHIP
MADE SIMPLE

ED OAKLEY
DOUG KRUG

LEADERSHIP
MADE SIMPLE

Inquiries regarding permission for use of the material contained in this book should be addressed to:

CornerStone Leadership Institute
P.O. Box 764087
Dallas, TX 75376
888.789.LEAD

Printed in the United States of America
ISBN: 0-9788137-5-8

Credits
Design, art direction, and production   Melissa Monogue, Back Porch Creative, Plano, TX
                                          info@BackPorchCreative.com
Copy Editor   Kathleen Green, Positively Proofed, Plano, TX
                                          info@PositivelyProofed.com

Advanced Praise for *Leadership Made Simple*

"You have simply captured the essence of leadership! What I find the most impressive about your book is the clarity and simplicity with which complex ideas are put forth – clarity that makes intuitive sense even to people without previous training in leadership."

> **Ms. Ariane David, Ph.D.**
> **Center for Organizational Excellence,**
> **National University**

"There's no need for aspiring leaders to search through hundreds of books on leadership, looking for a formula for success. Oakley & Krug have distilled it all into one brilliant, easy to master, five-step system that can make many seemingly impossible challenges instantly possible, and they've made it simple!"

> **Brian Lee, CSP**
> **Author, *Satisfaction Guaranteed: How to Satisfy Every Customer Every Time***

"Your examples and simple-yet-effective processes allowed me to immediately begin solving problems in my head as I read with forward focus."

> **Dr. Kevin D. Gazzara**
> **Strategy & Design Program Manager**
> **Intel Corporation**

"… incredibly meaningful because those reading it can grasp your principles and put them into action immediately."

> **Pamela J. Holland**
> **COO**
> **Brody Communications**

"I am inspired by your book! I can clearly see how your simple, yet vital process will increase the quality of, and buy-in for, the plan."

> **Ralph Johnson**
> **Project Manager**
> **IBM Global Services**

"The 'five magic questions' of the Framework for Leadership are so flexible and creative that they can be used at every level of an organization with astonishing success."

> H. Joseph Marshall, Ph.D.
> Managing Partner
> Resource Management of Boston

"This book is a breath of fresh air! Even the busiest of leaders can make time for this."

> Beverly Kaye
> CEO/Founder: Career Systems International
> Co-Author, *Love 'Em or Lose 'Em: Getting Good People to Stay*

"The Framework for Leadership will certainly help us in the development of future leaders. It has already worked for me!"

> Dave Malenfant
> Vice President, Global Supply Chain
> Alcon Laboratories

"*Leadership Made Simple* is excellent! I like the examples throughout. It's a winner!"

> Nido Qubein
> President, High Point University
> Chairman, Great Harvest Bread Company

"This book demystifies what it takes to be a leader. Very well done."

> Ken Banks
> CEO, KAB Marketing
> Seminole, FL

"Effective communications is vital within and between organizations and their stakeholders. This excellent book provides a powerful framework for making that happen smoothly."

> Jeff Julin, President
> MGA Communications

"Leadership generally defies description, however, the book reminds us that it need not be mystical, or something that one is born to alone. It can be learned."

Stuart Ochiltree
Chairman, Univera Life Sciences

"THE key tool that every small-business owner needs to help him/her bridge the gap between just managing and really leading. Read it today."

Carol Bergmann
Author, *Managing Your Energy at Work:*
The Key to Unlocking Hidden Potential in
the Workplace

"Einstein said the hardest part of discovering the Theory of Relativity was 'determining how to think about it.' He was seeking a framework from which to explore the information that could lead him to his goal. *Leadership Made Simple* is such a tool."

Jim Cathcart, Author, *Relationship Selling*
Founder, 101 Leaders Alliance

"*Leadership Made Simple* is awesome! The Framework for Leadership™ provides accountability without pointing fingers, and the whole process starts with celebrating successes, a perfect fit for the Starbucks culture. Every manager should read it and live it!"

Lindsey Braun,
Assistant Store Manager

TABLE OF CONTENTS

Introduction   9

Chapter 1 –   The Simple Truth About Leadership   13

Chapter 2 –   The Foundation of Simplicity: 19
              The Answers are in the Room

Chapter 3 –   The Framework for Leadership: 23
              Forward Focus and Effective Questions

Chapter 4 –   Step 1: Success Breeds Success   33

Chapter 5 –   Step Two: Analyze Success   41

Chapter 6 –   Step Three: Clarify the Goal   49

Chapter 7 –   Step Four: Establish Benefits   57

Chapter 8 –   Step Five: Plan and Take Action   65

Chapter 9 –   Putting It All Together –   75
              Goal Achievement

Chapter 10 – Examples of Framework for Leadership   81
              in Action

Chapter 11 – Sometimes It Can Be Even Simpler   91

Chapter 12 – Emotions in the Workplace   97

Chapter 13 – The Intention Behind the Questions   103

Appendix –   Questions for Specific Applications   111

About the Authors   116

Bring LMS Message to Your Team   117

INTRODUCTION

Simplicity is the ultimate sophistication.

– Leonardo da Vinci

How would you like to have a process to simplify many of your complex leadership challenges? What if there was a simple way to:

♦ Manage change initiatives.

♦ Create buy-in among many stakeholders.

♦ Solve both simple and complex problems.

♦ Establish shared visions.

♦ Determine breakthrough growth strategies.

♦ Resolve conflicts between people and teams.

The book you are holding provides you with a systematic process to do all the above ... and more.

For nearly two decades, we've had the privilege of working with many leaders and their teams from all levels in organizations, large and small. We have been teaching and utilizing our Framework for Leadership™ as a simple tool for dealing with leadership and management challenges.

Regardless of the circumstances ... from complicated process solutions to development programs to specific workshops ... we have trusted this simple process, even when we could not predict how it would lead to the outcomes being sought. Yet, time after time, the process worked. Often the solutions were spontaneous, incremental improvements and many times they were gradual and transformational improvements.

The principles described in this book naturally shift participants from problem-orientation to solutions-orientation. This simple but profound shift works when the situation may seem the most challenging ... even impossible. The principles outlined in this book will help create a communicative, collaborative environment where solutions will evolve from the people closest to the issue. You will see specific examples of how the Framework for Leadership has worked in other organizations.

Leadership Made Simple provides a practical, easy-to-use process that will help you produce immediate, tangible, real-world results. You will also discover

> *Leadership Made Simple* provides a practical, easy-to-use process that will help you produce immediate, tangible, real-world results.

how to optimize results by balancing and integrating the systems/ processes and the people/talent aspects of your business.

We encourage you to begin applying these principles today!

"The basis of leadership is the capacity of the leader to change the mindset, the framework of the other person."

– Warren Bennis

Footnote: Some of the examples were facilitated by only one of the authors. For ease of reading, we have used the term "I" or "we" throughout the book.

THE SIMPLE TRUTH ABOUT LEADERSHIP

"I knew then and believe even more firmly now –
there is a simpler way to lead organizations, one that requires
less effort and produces less stress than the current practices."

– Meg Wheatley, Ph.D.

Some of us have been deceived into thinking leadership is a complicated, mysterious and elusive ability only a few special people possess. That is simply not true. In fact, leadership is something virtually everyone provides at certain times, and because of this universality, leadership must be simple in order to succeed.

So why does leadership often appear so complex? Because the challenge is to effectively manage important processes while leading people … all at the same time.

Every organizational process has its "hard" part – managing things – and its "soft" part – leading people. The hard part includes structures, systems, procedures, processes, policies, protocols, plans, tools, etc. The soft part involves people – their creativity, attitudes, energy, focus, emotions, buy-in, resistance, fears and level of trust … or lack thereof.

Traditional management has concentrated on the hard components, while traditional leadership has focused on the soft ones. To be completely effective, you must do both – manage *things* and lead your *people* – and the people part is usually the more challenging of the two.

> To be completely effective, you must do both – manage *things* and lead your *people* – and the people part is usually the more challenging of the two.

We surveyed managers from more than 65 countries and hundreds of companies with the same question: "Which is more difficult – the hard part (managing processes and things) or the soft part (leading people)?"

Regardless of culture or country, the answer was almost always the same: "The soft part."

Surprising? Of course not!

Almost without exception, the main issues within organizations involve miscommunication among people.

However, most management training is typically focused on managing processes. Very little time is devoted to the skills and techniques needed to lead individual employees or teams. No wonder so many struggle with leadership!

This is not to say management should take a back seat to leadership or the soft aspect is more important than the hard. On the contrary, each is critical to managing effectively. What's important is maintaining balance between both sides. Focusing on one part and ignoring the other is the perfect formula for chaos … or worse.

Strong management skills are not enough when you need to cope with change, your organization is in transition or you need to discover new directions so your company can thrive (or just survive). A balanced blend of management and leadership is usually needed to provide inspiration and motivation to bring out the best in people.

So, how do you lead effectively? One thing is clear – it must be simple or it's not likely to work.

The Power of Simplicity

In his excellent book, *The Power of Simplicity*, best-selling author Jack Trout said, "… business is not that complex. It's just that there are too many people out there making it complex. The way to fight complexity is to use simplicity."

That's our approach to leadership … the power of simplicity.

A few years ago we tested the power of simplicity while working in an oil field production unit in Indonesia where English was the typical manager's *third* language. We facilitated all the sessions in English without translation and quietly wondered if our clients really understood the Framework for Leadership process we were explaining. Or, if they did understand, would they be able to apply it in real-world situations. We were testing the power of simplicity!

Fortunately, they impressed us with the quality of their planning, problem-solving, creativity and solutions to real challenges. They did it all using our Framework for Leadership outlined in this book.

As a testimony to the success, John Baltz, then vice president of the unit, left an urgent phone message that awaited our return to the United States.

John had been a member of a small group that had used the Framework for Leadership in a real-life situation during the workshop. The process was so valuable, he wanted to share the results with VP's of other divisions. He was calling to see where we had stored the easel charts for the exercise, so he could tell about the process and share the results with the other executives.

> Even the most complex aspects of leadership can be simplified.

John was impressed with what he had discovered ... that even the most complex aspects of leadership *can* be simplified ... and that is the simple truth about leadership.

Measurable Successes

Following are three examples of measurable success achieved by using the tools, concepts and attitudes explained in *Leadership Made Simple*:

♦ A regional claim center of a major insurance company was in big trouble. With its customer service rating at a miserable 58 percent, a senior manager was brought in to lead a turnaround. Using the concepts and tools found in this book, he took a very simple approach to the project – so simple that, in the beginning, it generated naysaying and pushback from almost every quarter. Eighteen months later, the senior manager's approach was vindicated: the claim center's customer service rating had soared to 93 percent – making its program *the* benchmark for the rest of the company. The key to the effectiveness of his approach was simplicity.

♦ A.J. Hiltenbrand, former director of corporate executive development for a major pharmaceutical and surgical company, was determined to prove the bottom-line value of the soft-skills education his organization had provided for years. At the request of senior management, Hiltenbrand held workshops in which the *Leadership Made Simple* process was taught in markets in several foreign countries. As a result of the response to the workshop: the Italian market reported a 10-to-1 return on investment (ROI); in Greece, the figure was 9-to-1; and in Turkey, 13-to-1. Bulgaria reported a staggering 48-to-1 ROI, which included an extra $984,000 in accounts receivable collected because of decisions made using the process.

♦ Penny Weismuller, manager of disease control for a county in California, shared the tools provided in this book with her team to develop collaborative, innovative solutions for housing communicable tuberculosis patients – a very expensive and previously "complex" problem. The simple, creative ideas they generated maintained the required isolation while saving $206,277 the first three months and $285,824 during the next quarter. They anticipated similar savings, going forward. Imagine the impact on the "bottom line?"

The details of each of these examples will be discussed in later chapters. Simple is powerful!

"No matter how complicated a problem is,
it usually can be reduced to a simple,
comprehensible form which is often the best solution."
– An Wang, founder of Wang Labs

THE FOUNDATION OF SIMPLICITY: THE ANSWERS ARE IN THE ROOM

"Leaders do not need to have all the answers.
They do need to ask the right questions."
– Ronald Heifitz and Donald Laurie
Harvard Business Review, February 2000

Leaders don't have all the answers … and they shouldn't be expected to. But when you access the creativity, knowledge, wisdom and spirit of your people, the answers are available within the organization. The experts are already there! The key is accessing those solutions.

Recently, I – along with 22 other professional speakers – was awaiting a presentation on intellectual property rights, when I noticed the host kept ducking in and out of the room.

Bob Wendover, a friend, author and speaker, did *not* look happy, so I followed him out of the room and asked if I could help.

"The speaker is 30 minutes late," Bob explained, "and I can't get in touch with him. I think we're out of luck, because it appears he's not going to show up!"

With nothing to lose, I proposed an idea – and Bob agreed to let me run the meeting.

"I believe the 'answers are in the room,'" I told the group as I began, "and I would like to test that belief." Then, I asked the attendees to write down any questions they had about intellectual property rights.

After the questions were collected, I read the first one, and asked, "Who has the answer to this question?" Three people raised their hands and addressed the question.

I moved to the next question and again asked who had the answer? Several people responded.

This process continued for more than an hour until all but one question had been answered. The room was buzzing with energy.

Despite the absence of the expert, the meeting was a phenomenal success – or perhaps the success came *because* of his absence. If the attorney had shown up, he might have: (A) put half the audience to sleep and (B) withheld specifics when asked detailed questions (details often require a significant consultation fee). After all, the attorney may have agreed to speak, at least partially, for his own marketing purposes.

To the benefit and surprise of those attending the meeting – and as my hypothesis suggested – the answers were in the room, the same dynamic that has proven itself over and over in the last two decades.

Letting Go for the Best Solution

A good leader recognizes he or she doesn't have – and doesn't need to have – the answer for every challenge encountered by the team. This acknowledgement releases an ego-driven desire to be the front of all knowledge.

As a second step, the leader launches a search for the best answer, knowing that leadership isn't about dispensing wisdom but, instead, about harnessing team members' unique creativity, experiences and ideas to produce results. These results, ultimately, are greater than the sum of the individual abilities, and create exceptional, even transformational, results.

Author of the popular business novel, *The Goal*, Eli Goldratt said, "If you want people to take action, you must refrain from giving them the answers." Goldratt also must have known, "The experts are already in the room!"

> "The experts are already in the room!"

But, for this to happen, a manager, first, has to *believe* that the team *does* have the answers … and then take action based on that belief. For some managers, this might require a leap of faith, especially for those who have created teams that depend on him/her for direction and answers.

The next step is inviting the answers and the solutions by asking the right questions.

When Dennis Wagner trusted the "answers were in the room" for the federal government's organ donation initiative, his team achieved more progress in 15 months than in the previous 10 years. Because Dennis had worked with us on other projects, he believed the answers to their challenges lay with the people who were already part of the initiative – not just his own people, but all the people involved.

In an unprecedented move, he and his team brought together many of the stakeholders – hospital administrators and CEOs, many of the 59 organ procurement organizations, cardiologists and emergency room nurses – to discuss challenges and potential solutions.

At large "town hall" meetings across the U.S., the various groups identified specific problems they faced. Then these same stakeholders were asked if anyone had addressed, or even solved, those problems. *In every case*, at least one person or organization (often several) had developed a solution for a particular issue that had been brought up.

Essentially, they had already created best-practice solutions for each of the problems and only had to share the specifics. Thanks to people who were already involved, Dennis knew that finding the answers was just a matter of asking the right questions. The conferences were a resounding success.

Although finding the answers was important, just as important was *who* supplied those answers. When the stakeholders *themselves* pinpoint the solutions, they are highly motivated to make the innovations work. How could they not "buy in" to their own ideas? How could they let their own ideas fail?

Leadership Made Simple:
The answers are in the room ...

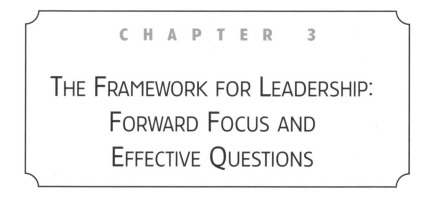

THE FRAMEWORK FOR LEADERSHIP: FORWARD FOCUS AND EFFECTIVE QUESTIONS

"All of life's answers are available,
if we just knew what questions to ask."

– Albert Einstein

Forward Focus is looking at what is working in the current situation, discovering where you want to go and strategizing how to move forward.

Rather than overly focusing energy and attention on what didn't work and who's to blame, Forward Focus shifts attention to what *did* work, who to acknowledge, what's the solution and what we *can* do to move forward.

Most people cannot effectively focus on two things simultaneously. If you consistently look backward, it's impossible to focus on the tasks ahead. As illustrated by the graphic on the following page, when the focus is on the obstacles in your path, your attention becomes mired in those obstacles and prevents you from looking for ways to move toward your goals. That's backward focus.

Forward Focus is continually focusing on where you want to go. Your energy is spent on how to get there in order to achieve your chosen objectives with maximum efficiency. Along the way, of course, you continually deal with any challenges keeping you from achieving your goal. You certainly do not ignore them.

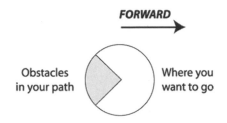

Another example of backward vs. Forward Focus is the choice between "all the reasons why we cannot" accomplish a goal vs. "how we can" as illustrated below.

The difference is clear when we phrase the choice this way, but it's easy to slip back into the mindset of "reasons we cannot achieve the goal." If you embrace these reasons and this focus, you cannot accomplish your goal. You can only accomplish a task if you focus on the ways you can get it done.

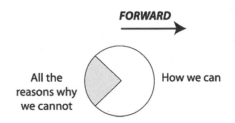

Creative thinkers tend to focus their energy on where they want to go. When they drift off course, they keep coming back to that focus. As a result, they get there more quickly, because they continually seek solutions.

Reactive thinkers often focus on obstacles and problems, getting stuck on the backward focus side. This prevents them from reaching their goals or, at minimum, this negative focus slows their progress and wastes precious energy.

Forward Focus distinguishes the subtle-but-profound difference between focusing on problems and focusing on solutions, as illustrated below.

The reality is that to identify a problem, you have to focus on it. In order to keep moving forward, though, it is important to quickly move to the solution side and not get bogged down in what caused the problem and who was to blame.

What you most want to know is how to solve it and how to prevent it from happening again.

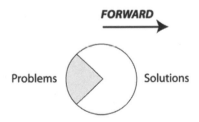

Forward Focus is a simple but powerful principle that keeps you moving toward achieving your objectives.

When our focus is on what's not working, we become paralyzed. When we use Forward Focus – on what *is* working and the successes we have already achieved – we release our creativity and are ready to reach higher and innovate more.

> Shifting from a backward focus to a Forward Focus fundamentally alters the mindset of the people in an organization.

Shifting from a backward focus to a Forward Focus fundamentally alters the mindset of the people in an organization. By highlighting their successes you invite creativity and new possibilities. It's no surprise when organizations and individuals direct more energy *toward* their objectives they reach those objectives more quickly.

Here is an example of what Forward Focus brings to the table. A Georgia-Pacific plant was going through an ISO 9002 certification, for which they had worked hard and long. When the auditors completed their assessment, they told the director of quality, "Congratulations! You've passed the audit with such flying colors, we don't even need to do a debrief with your organization. There really aren't enough issues to mention."

The QA director responded, "*We do* want a debriefing. I want to get our entire organization together, and I want you to tell our people all the specific ways they have done such a good job." The auditors had been so focused on finding what was not right, they hadn't considered the value of sharing the good practices they had discovered.

When the auditors debriefed and told the great success stories about the Georgia-Pacific plant, the energy and enthusiasm was powerful! People are energized when they hear praise for things they've worked so hard to accomplish.

This isn't to say you should ignore problems and place zero focus on them. We're merely suggesting that there's greater power in shifting the *balance* toward Forward Focus and *how* we deal with problems, once they arise.

So, if the answers are in the room and Focusing Forward generates creativity, what's the secret to getting people to more consistently shift their Focus Forward? It simply begins with the leader asking the right questions.

Introducing Effective Questions

An Effective Question is the "right" question – one that helps identify solutions to achieve the desired results.

How many times have you asked, "Why are we behind schedule?" and received blank stares and head scratching?

Do questions such as, "Who made that decision?" provoke arguments and finger pointing?

If you are like most leaders, you've asked these or similar questions before … and endured all-of-the-above negative reactions.

These are *ineffective* questions. They are negative and backward-focused, causing people to "circle the wagons" in defensiveness instead of creating and testing ideas and solutions.

An ineffective question causes your team to concentrate on what's wrong and who's to blame. These questions drain energy, destroy trust, and encourage a "cover-your-butt" mentality. Instead of thinking, "What can we do to move forward?" the team thinks, "How can I answer that question without getting blamed for the problem?"

Effective Questions

So, given the above, what are *Effective* Questions?

> Nothing redirects people's thinking better than a well-phrased question.

Effective Questions are the single most potent leadership tool we know. Nothing redirects people's thinking better than a well-phrased question.

Effective Questions create a mindset shift away from problem-orientation and limitations. They move your team forward toward solution-orientation and possibilities.

Phil Schwartz experienced this shift when he spearheaded developing a major report to be issued under the signature of the head of a large federal agency. It was Friday morning when he suddenly realized the introduction and context-setting chapter had not been done.

The report was due at 8 a.m. Monday, and the task seemed impossible.

Phil went to Paul, his boss, who had recently been introduced to the Leadership Framework. When he saw Phil's panic, Paul completely shifted his concern by asking four Effective Questions:

- ♦ What options do you have?
- ♦ What resources are available?
- ♦ What can you do to augment resources?
- ♦ What help do you need?

Each of these questions focus forward ... and, notice, each of these questions are open-ended and stimulate thought. None can be answered with a simple "yes" or "no."

Open-ended questions invite people to elaborate without being prompted. This increases the value of the conversation because they make people think.

Thanks to the clear thinking these open-ended questions inspired, Phil not only met his deadline, but during its final review, the entire report required only minor changes. He nailed it on the first draft!

Imagine the difference in outcomes if Paul's questions had been backward focused.

Suppose one of your team members gives you all the reasons he can't make his deadline. He's stuck in a backward-focused rut. What would happen if you asked, "What would it take to finish on time?" or "What ideas do you have for getting back on track?"

Maybe you'd be greeted with silence – at first. But if the person actually attempted to answer your questions, he would *have to shift* his focus from "reasons why he couldn't" to "resources that he needed to get things done" or "actions to move forward."

He'd have to shift his thinking from the obstacles to the solutions ... and that shift would dramatically impact his results.

Quality of the Answers

The quality of your questions determines the quality of responses you get.

For example, if you want to improve a process, you might ask, "What ideas do you have for improving this process?" which is very different from the more typical question "What are the problems with this process?"

If you want to enhance productivity, you can ask, "What could we do to make our productivity even better?" vs. "What is stopping us from being more productive?"

In both of these examples, the differences are subtle but profound. Forward Focused, open-ended questions uncover answers that "are already in the room." We're not suggesting Effective Questions will always produce instant results, but given time, they *will produce results*. They optimize the situation.

What questions would you most like answered right now by:

- ♦ Your team?
- ♦ An individual team member?
- ♦ A family member?
- ♦ Yourself?

Take a moment to jot down some of those questions in the space below.

- ♦ Open each with the words "what" or "how."
- ♦ Next, make sure they are Forward Focused.
- ♦ Then, ask the Effective Questions of the appropriate people, and trust that the answer(s) will come – in their own time.

_____

_____

_____

_____

_____

PRACTICAL SOLUTIONS TO YOUR
GREATEST MANAGEMENT CHALLENGES

LEADERSHIP
MADE SIMPLE

"Simplicity is the
ultimate sophistication."
— Leonardo da Vinci

ED OAKLEY
DOUG KRUG

3 Easy Ways to Order Copies for Your Management Team!

1. **Complete the order form on back and fax to 972-274-2884**

2. **Visit www.CornerStoneLeadership.com**

3. **Call 1-888-789-LEAD (5323)**

CornerStone
Leadership Institute

The Next Level ... Leading Beyond the Status Quo provides insight and direction on what it takes to lead your team to a higher and greater Next Level. **$14.95**

Power Exchange – How to Boost Accountability & Performance in Today's Workforce offers practical strategies to help any leader boost accountability and performance in today's workforce. **$9.95**

Monday Morning Communications provides workable strategies to solving serious communications challenges. **$14.95**

Passionate Performance ... Engaging Minds and Hearts to Conquer the Competition offers practical strategies to engage the minds and heart of your team at home, work, church or community. Read it and conquer your competition! **$9.95**

180 Ways to Walk the Recognition Talk will help you provide recognition to your people more often and more effectively. **$9.95**

I Quit, But Forgot to Tell You provides the straightforward, logical truths that lead to disengagement ... and provides the antidotes to prevent the virus from spreading within your organization. **$14.95**

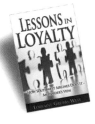

Lessons in Loyalty takes you inside Southwest Airlines to discover what makes it so different ... and successful. **$14.95**

The Manager's Coaching Handbook is a practical guide to improve performance from your superstars, middle stars and falling stars. **$9.95**

Visit www.CornerStoneLeadership.com for additional books and resources.

nce Package $149.95

Start Right – Stay Right
is every employee's
straighttalk guide to
personal responsibility
and job success. Perfect
for every employee at
every level. **$9.95**

**The Manager's
Communication
Handbook** will allow
you to connect with
employees and create
the understanding,
support and
acceptance critical
to your success.
$9.95

**Ouch! that Stereotype
Hurts** is a guide to
show you how to present
information and lead
discussions in ways
that include everyone
and avoid bias,
stereotyping, or potential
discrimination. **$12.95**

**The NEW CornerStone
Perpetual Calendar**, a
compelling collection
of quotes about
leadership and life,
is perfect for office
desks, school and
home countertops.
Offering a daily dose
of inspiration, this
terrific calendar
makes the perfect
gift or motivational
reward. **$14.95**

The CornerStone Leadership Collection of Cards is designed to make it easy for
you to show appreciation for your team, clients and friends. The awesome
photography and your personal message written inside will create a lasting impact.
Pack/12 (12 styles/1 each) **$24.95**
Posters also available.

**One of each of the items shown here are included
in the *Accelerate Team Performance* Package!**

Order Form

1-30 copies $14.95	31-99 copies $13.95	100+ copies $12.95

Leadership Made Simple	____ copies X _____ = $ ____

Leadership Made Simple Companion Resources

PowerPoint® Presentation (downloadable)　　　____ copies X $99.95　= $ ____

Additional Team Performance Resources

Accelerate Team Performance Package　　　____ pack(s) X $149.95　= $ ____
(Includes all items shown inside.)

Other Books

_____　　____ copies X _____ = $ ____

_____　　____ copies X _____ = $ ____

_____　　____ copies X _____ = $ ____

Shipping & Handling　　　$ ____

Subtotal　　　$ ____

Sales Tax (8.25%-TX Only)　$ ____

Total (U.S. Dollars Only)　$ ____

Shipping and Handling Charges

Total $ Amount	Up to $49	$50-$99	$100-$249	$250-$1199	$1200-$2999	$3000+
Charge	$6	$9	$16	$30	$80	$125

Name _____ Job Title _____

Organization _____ Phone _____

Shipping Address _____ Fax _____

Billing Address _____ Email _____
(required when ordering PowerPoint® Presentation)

City _____ State _____ ZIP _____

❑ Please invoice (Orders over $200) Purchase Order Number (if applicable) _____

Charge Your Order:　❑ MasterCard　　❑ Visa　　❑ American Express

Credit Card Number _____ Exp. Date _____

Signature _____

❑ Check Enclosed (Payable to: CornerStone Leadership)

Fax　972.274.2884
Phone　888.789.5323　　　www.**CornerStoneLeadership**.com　　　**P.O. Box 764087**
Dallas, TX 75376

Specific Effective Questions

The next chapter introduces the first of a series of specific questions to help you elicit answers to your greatest management challenges. These flexible and powerful questions create the Framework for Leadership.

"Those who plan the battle are less likely to battle the plan."

– Dwight D. Eisenhower

STEP ONE ... SUCCESS BREEDS SUCCESS

"What is impossible to do in one paradigm
can be easy in the next."
– Joel Barker

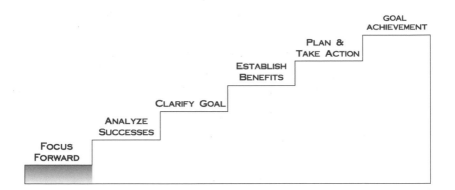

Key Question: What is already working?

A paper manufacturing plant was in serious jeopardy of closing. Operating 24/7, the plant was losing money. The more paper they made, the more money they lost. It seemed just a matter of time before the plant would have to cease operations.

We were called into consult in one last attempt to turn around a difficult situation.

Jennavieve Joshua introduced the Framework for Leadership and facilitated the management team through the process. She set the context before beginning: "I realize the challenging situation in which you find yourself. I realize everyone's job is on the line. I also know there are many problems. Knowing that, I want to encourage you to fully participate in looking at your situation from a different perspective.

"I would like to use the Framework for Leadership as our guide. Let's experience the process, and see what happens."

She stood at a flip chart to capture input and said, "What are some of the things you believe are actually working? What successes are you having, no matter how small?"

The response was underwhelming. Silence was, by far, the strongest input. But Jennavieve had "been there before" and encouraged everyone to look at even their smallest successes.

The participants, eventually, were divided into smaller groups to change the dynamics since she knew this question was a critical first step in moving toward potential solutions.

Finally, she was offered a few seemingly insignificant comments about successes – almost reluctantly. Slowly, there was a small shift in energy as individuals began to participate and more significant successes were shared. Before long, most of the team members were contributing positive perspectives.

The ideas generated increased buy-in for the process.

A few significant realizations came out that were not known by the majority, and one specific success surprised many in the group because none of them knew about it.

The first step of the Framework for Leadership, "What is already working?" was key to shifting the group's energy and focus to the *possibility* of keeping the plant open.

This first question was the critical preparatory step to get the people Forward Focused.

The creativity pump was primed, and now people were ready to propose ideas about next steps, leveraging earlier successes and achieving new goals – ultimately keeping the plant open and saving the local economy.

They were moving forward, slowly, but forward nevertheless.

"What successes are we having?" or "What is already working?"

One question made all the difference. The quality of answers we get depends upon the quality of questions we ask.

The paper plant is typical of the difference you can make when you open a meeting – any kind of meeting – with Step 1 questions, "What's already working?" "Where have we been successful?" "What are our strengths?" "Where are we making progress?"

> The quality of answers we get depends upon the quality of questions we ask.

These types of questions imply, "We want to focus on leveraging our current successes to achieve our goals."

This communications tool may be simple, but it has many applications because it affects people on a variety of psychological and emotional levels and eventually redirects the group dynamic into positive and productive thinking.

Don't mistake "simplicity" with "simplistic" or "simple-minded." You may be tempted to think, "This is a Pollyannaish kind of question and would never work in our culture."

Okay … so maybe you'll get a few blank stares or ready quips the first time you employ the approach, but that will change when people witness how Effective Questions shift the focus from backward to forward, from negative to positive, achieving tangible results. (*Note*: "EQ" will be used as shorthand for Effective Question(s), going forward in our story.)

Benefits From Step 1 Questions

◆ *A baseline of success is established.* Looking at what is already successful provides a benchmark, laying the foundation from which to build.

◆ *The energy level is raised.* It should come as no surprise … when people start discussing their successes, they get excited. Appreciating being acknowledged for their role in shaping those successes, they'll want to contribute to future achievements by making suggestions, sharing ideas, and collaborating with teammates.

> There is a natural relationship between creative energy and a positive environment.

◆ *Creativity is boosted.* There is a natural relationship between creative energy and a positive environment. Why? Because a negative environment tends to squelch creativity, while a positive one enhances it.

♦ *Focus is shifted from problems to solutions.* It's important to identify what isn't working and why. Don't ignore problems, but use a Forward Focus approach to problem-solving to get the positive results you want.

♦ *Defensiveness is eliminated.* Backward focus diminishes – even invalidates – their hard work, their competence and their accomplishments. Forward Focus values them.

♦ *Resistance to change is broken down.* When people are acknowledged for what they are already doing well, they are naturally more open to doing things differently.

♦ *Self-confidence is built.* Self-confidence is a major factor in a person's performance. That being the case, which tactic is more likely to build an employee's self-confidence: acknowledging and focusing on what's being done right, or pointing out what's being done wrong? People are more likely to believe they can achieve a major goal when you build their confidence. This is done by focusing – at the very beginning – on what they've already achieved instead of pointing out flaws and mistakes.

♦ *Trust is built.* When people are asked what they've done that's working, what they are doing *right* – it alters their self-perception. Over time, they begin to think differently about what's right with them instead of what's wrong, and as they begin to trust themselves, self-confidence is gained as they realize they really *do* have answers.

Modifying the Question to Fit the Situation

There are as many ways to phrase the Step 1 Effective Questions as there are applications for the Framework.

Michelle Brown, customer service manager at a large plastics manufacturer, put a new spin on the Step 1 Effective Question as soon as she returned to work from a session with one of our facilitators.

"Michelle, we've got an irate customer," said her colleagues. "Here's the information. You've got to call this guy!"

She thought, "I'd like to start by asking the customer what's already working, but, to say the least, that could come off as self-serving. How can I re-word the question and still take advantage of the concept?"

The solution came to her quickly.

When she phoned the customer, she immediately gave him the opportunity to vent about the problem – a key part of her process. Once his negativity had dissipated, she asked, "Mr. Thompson, what have other vendors done in this situation that's worked well for you?"

A stunned Mr. Thompson collected his thoughts and answered her. Then Michelle said, "Okay, if we did that within the next few days, would it satisfy you?"

He said it would. She implemented the solution and gained a very satisfied customer.

The key to the turnaround was a nicely adapted "what's working?" question.

Regardless of the situation or circumstances, the primary benefit of the Step 1 EQ is that it causes you to focus on what you did well. It takes the focus away from what went wrong. This step applies to the individual as well as group efforts.

You can also ask *yourself* these questions to stimulate your own creativity and problem-solving abilities.

Over the years, we've received calls from many clients who have spent entire meetings focusing on just the first step of the Framework, because the question sparked so much learning and energy that resulted in solutions. Ultimately, this energy and learning positively impacted progress.

The first step Effective Question is just *that* – effective – because success breeds continued success.

What is already working?

What successes are we having?

Where do we agree?

What are some things you appreciate about the situation?

What have we done successfully in similar situations?

What do you appreciate or respect about the person (or relationship)?

What went well this week?

"Success produces success, just as money produces money."
– Nicolas de Chamfort

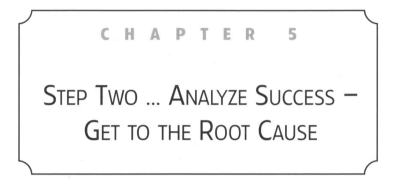

CHAPTER 5

STEP TWO ... ANALYZE SUCCESS – GET TO THE ROOT CAUSE

The success combination in business is:
Do what you do better ... and ... Do more of what you do.

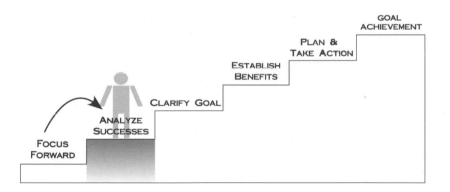

Key Question: What is making it work? Or ... What caused this success?

The second step of the Framework for Leadership is to learn from successes so they can be repeated. This also builds more creative energy while acknowledging people for their contributions to these successes.

The "What makes it work?" question is designed to facilitate a root-cause analysis of a success — yours or someone else's. If you hope to duplicate and build on prior achievements, your next step is finding out *why* something succeeded.

Unfortunately, many people become fixated on understanding the causes of failure. They become experts in incompetence but remain unconscious about what drives their organization's success.

> Understanding the cause of failure is important. Understanding the cause of success is far more powerful!

Understanding the cause of failure is important. Understanding the cause of success is far more powerful!

Remember how Dennis Wagner and his team led an initiative to generate a stunning increase in the number of organs available for transplant? They did so by finding "the answers in the room."

Exactly *how* they found those answers brings us to Step 2 of the Leadership Framework — analyzing success.

When Wagner took the reins, he noticed only about 200 out of 5,800 hospitals were achieving adequate donation rates whereas 50 percent of the potential donors actually donated their organs.

If every hospital were to achieve that same rate, nobody — *nobody* — would die for lack of an organ.

At that time, 88,000 people were on waiting lists, and 17 people died each day in need of an organ. That's when Wagner realized the issue wasn't a lack of organs. The problem was an inefficient donor system. Every day, people with usable organs were being buried alongside those who might have lived – had they received one of those usable organs.

Wagner's first question was, "What are these 200 successful hospitals doing differently?"

The initial answer was, "We don't know. We've been trying to find out what the other 5,600 hospitals are doing wrong."

Let's be clear. These were not bad people … or hospitals. They were just stuck in the "find the problem and fix it" mindset.

Having worked with Effective Questions (EQ's) for years, Wagner clearly understood the value of building on successes, not problems.

Two cities had donation rates much higher than the average – Houston, Texas and Madison, Wisconsin.

Dennis contacted their Organ Procurement Organizations (OPO's) to discover why they were so successful. Once again, the response was, "We don't know."

These two OPO's were simply doing what they normally did, and it happened to be working. They didn't realize other OPO's were not as successful or that they, themselves, had pioneered a uniquely successful model – until they were asked.

Upon closer examination, one discovery was, in those two cities, the OPO coordinators were assigned to specific hospitals. They remained on site at the primary hospitals on a 24/7 basis, instead of having to be paged when needed. This allowed them to develop relationships with families early in life-threatening circumstances.

These relationships made it much easier to ask for organ donations if death became imminent.

A simple question – which analyzed the OPO's current success – produced answers the less successful hospitals could use to make their organ programs more productive.

By asking the right questions, Wagner's team discovered the factors of a successful model and introduced it to Organ Procurement Organizations throughout the country. This and other successful practices eventually produced amazing results in very little time. Since that time, new records are being set, monthly, in the number of organs being donated.

Imagine the excitement as team members in the various hospitals and OPO's learned how and why things were working elsewhere. That information provided solutions to long-standing problems, which generated tremendous enthusiasm and boosted everyone's creativity ... and morale.

Although the donation programs, themselves, are fascinating, what's more important to understand is the process that created their success – a process beginning when you ask the Step 2 Effective Question:

What is the cause of this success?
Or, **What, specifically, makes it work?**

The goal of analyzing success in the Step 2 of the Leadership Framework is to bring people from unconscious competence – not knowing why they are successful – to conscious competence, or being fully aware of why they are successful.

If we don't know why we've succeeded, we can't learn from those successes and we can't transfer this knowledge to others.

Sadly, this concept is frequently "missing in action" in corporate America. When we achieve a success, our tendency is usually to acknowledge the victory and say, "Next."

One large computer company prides itself on "celebrating for a nanosecond" before moving on. If they are moving so quickly, you can bet they are not taking time to learn from their successes ... and they're far less likely to repeat their successes if they don't take time to understand the causes for these successes. When a problem occurs, it's common for leaders to hit the "red alert" button and assemble all hands to analyze problems. Yet, these same leaders rarely call meetings to analyze their recent successes.

The real opportunity lies in analyzing their successes so these can be consistently repeated.

_____

The real opportunity lies in analyzing their successes so these can be consistently repeated.

_____

Remember the Wisconsin paper mill that was facing closure? When, "What is already working?" was facilitated, people were surprised that one particular shift – using one particular paper machine out of five – was more productive than all the rest.

Jennavieve, the facilitator, couldn't wait to ask, "What is that one team doing differently to be more productive?" (Notice that this is a variant of "What makes it work?")

The answer to that single question was not well known, but when the details surfaced, it showed the management team how to substantially improve productivity and keep the plant open.

Most of the plant *did not know* what that one team was doing to be more productive. Imagine the impact when 14 other teams implemented the strategy that was working so well for that team.

The result was that they stayed in business, saved their jobs and the local economy! Not bad for a simple little leadership process.

Step 2 of the Leadership Framework is important and analyzing success questions can be phrased in many ways:

- **What made it work?**

- **What is making it work?**

- **What, specifically, caused the success?**

- **To what do you attribute that success? What else?**

- **What did they do to accomplish that win?**

- **What made this situation different, so that the success was much greater?**

- **What did you do differently this time vs. last time to create a higher level of success?**

- **What did they do on a similar project that solved or prevented that problem?**

The wording isn't particularly important, as long as the focus is on understanding the details leading to the successes.

You have the opportunity to build a learning organization, because when people are running on solutions-oriented questions, learning happens naturally. When competence becomes conscious, it can be documented and duplicated.

By using Step 2 of the Framework, you can identify the transferable competencies and construct a process that can be employed by many others.

If your team has just had a big win, learn from it.

We often celebrate breakthroughs, but how often do we take time to dig down and understand how they came about? There are reasons for those successes. Be sure to understand what they are so you can duplicate them in the future.

> There are reasons for those successes. Be sure to understand what they are so you can duplicate them in the future.

Recently, I spoke to employees in a communication company who had just completed a very successful Information Technology project. They were taking the day off from normal work to celebrate an amazing success with a large, challenging project.

Having lunch with the project leader and noting the huge success, I asked the manager, "How much time did you spend at the end of the project to really understand what you and your people did to cause such an impressive success?"

She was silent for a few moments and then said enthusiastically, "That's a great idea!" – which meant they had not done it!

Whatever the situation, find solutions by building a learning collaborative – like the one used by the organ donation initiative – a model that brings people together to learn from one another. The focus is not on scrutinizing problems, but on learning about successful practices.

When you ask, "What made it work?" you begin searching for a common element: what someone or a team of people did well. But don't stop there. Use the process to probe deeper, to understand exactly *what* they did to be successful.

Everyone appreciates it when you tell them, "Good job," but often they aren't aware of what critical factors led to their success – *until you get them to really think about it*. That's why everyone benefits from Step 2 of the Framework.

That's also the root cause of why this question succeeds.

What made it work? *Or …*

What caused the success?

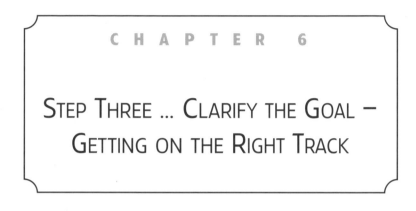

CHAPTER 6

STEP THREE ... CLARIFY THE GOAL – GETTING ON THE RIGHT TRACK

"The world stands aside to let anyone pass who knows where he is going."
– David Starr Jordan

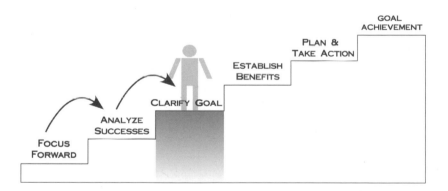

Key Question: What are we trying to accomplish? Or ... What is our objective?

Several years ago, *USA Today* reported on a recent survey about the main reasons teams fail, with the number one reason being "unclear goals" and number two, *"changing* goals."

In our consulting work, we often distribute a discovery questionnaire in advance of our interventions, processes or events, asking managers and their subordinates to define their current objectives.

Time after time, management lists one set of goals while the employees list another. People on different rungs of the organizational ladder often have different perspectives about directions and objectives.

The typical response from lower levels is, "It would really help if we had clear direction," while the response from higher levels is, usually, "Our direction is very clear."

Step 3 of the Framework, therefore, is to ask:

> **"What is our objective?"** *Or ...*
> **"What are we trying to accomplish?"**

This is an essential step for getting people onto the same, right track and moving in the same direction. After all, you can't expect everyone to arrive at the same destination if you haven't agreed where it is.

Why Isn't This Step 1 Instead of Step 3?

Sometimes we are asked, "Why isn't this question the first step of the Framework instead of the third? It seems like you need to *start* with the objective."

There is a certain amount of truth to that. To begin using the 5-step Framework, you have to have some idea of the objective ... and you do establish that, up front, as the context for why you're using this process.

After building the creative energy, though, we've found it extremely valuable to go back and look at the objective with new eyes. Often the result is an entirely different and more meaningful understanding of the objective.

Gaining alignment with a clear, shared goal is much easier when the foundation has been set with the first two Framework steps.

Let's look at an example of the importance of a clear objective.

The surgical manufacturing division of a Fortune 500 company was installing a new, enterprise-wide computer system. The project team was struggling with priorities. Because the project would impact everyone in the manufacturing environment, the project leader – Terri Martin, who is also controller of the facility – used the Framework for Leadership to plan the transition process.

When the team reached Step 3, however, they experienced a revelation. With the question, "What is our objective?" three different – and conflicting – objectives were uncovered, which had been put forth by three different stakeholders.

They soon realized the conflicting goals were making it difficult to establish priorities for moving forward, so the project team's first action was to resolve these conflicting goals among the stakeholders. Then, with the new clarity, they were able to focus on the appropriate priorities.

Avoidance and Distraction

In the absence of a clearly defined goal, people often shift to an "avoidance focus." But when the focus is on avoiding mistakes,

> In the absence of a clearly defined goal, people often shift to an "avoidance focus."

we actually gravitate toward those mistakes. Without any concrete *do's*, we steer straight for the *do nots*.

Avoiding doesn't work! What we try to avoid is the very thing our attention and action go toward.

Because of the natural tendency to focus on what we want to avoid, leadership needs to pull the team back to the actual goal. Therefore, it is vital for goals and objectives to be stated positively.

The goal of "increasing sales" is not the same as "don't lose sales." Step 3 of the Framework helps bring us back on track and keep us there. "What is our goal here?" "What are we trying to accomplish?"

It's also natural for people to become distracted in the workplace. We're not referring to the person who plays computer games or surfs the Internet instead of working, but the average person who gets distracted by various tasks, phone calls, personal issues, e-mails, interruptions, etc.

These people often lose clarity about what's important because distractions cause them to lose sight of what they're doing … and why they're doing it. They become more reactive than proactive.

Instead of focusing on the questions "What's my objective?" or "What is the best use of my time?" or "What are my priorities?" a person might think, "How do I get through the day?" or "How could I possibly get all this done?" He/she makes decisions based on the moment instead of the stated objective, disconnecting from the larger goal.

When Ed Tate approached the final rounds of the Toastmasters' world speaking competition, it seemed *everybody* was giving him advice about what *not* to do, and he was listening! Then it suddenly struck him. "Wait a minute! I don't want to focus on what *not* to do. That's like focusing on the very thing I don't want. I need to focus on what I *do* want."

At that point, he shifted his strategy and started asking previous winners what they had done to become champions.

Using the question, "What did you do to win?" he discovered what he needed to know about how to succeed. The answer wasn't about what *not* to do. It was about what *to* do.

Now he had a clear vision of what it took to win, and he did. Ed Tate became Toastmasters 2000 World Champion, beating out 20,000 contestants!

He's also confident a significant factor in his success was shifting focus away from "what not to do" and toward "what he wanted to do." Achieving clarity around an objective is critical.

In Support of Ownership

Although your people may be clear about the goal, you won't accomplish much without their ownership. Therefore, it's a good idea to get people involved in establishing the objective – whenever possible. If everyone has a say in molding the objective, you are more assured of buy-in.

> Although your people may be clear about the goal, you won't accomplish much without their ownership.

As district manager of Hewlett Packard, I asked colleague Lee Blackstone for advice on how to set quotas for the salespeople on my team.

Lee suggested I assemble my salespeople in a room and tell them what the quota would be for the entire team. Then, the team would have the rest of the day to figure out individual targets, which had to add up to the district total. In other words, leave it up to the team members to establish individual goals.

Of course, they knew if they were unable to accomplish the task by the end of the day, quotas would be assigned to them.

I saw nothing to lose, and put the idea in motion. The results were amazing. Near the end of the day, the salespeople approached me and said: "Okay. We're ready to talk."

I sat down with the team and each person declared his/her individual quota, taking responsibility and ownership for his/her goal.

I asked how they all felt about their quotas and, in every case, team members responded by saying the targets were fair and reasonable.

Some people assigned themselves lower quotas than I would have given, but others accepted higher targets. In most cases, senior people took on more responsibility to show their commitment to the team and their support of the new people.

By allowing the salespeople to establish their own specific and measurable objectives, we created a tremendous level of ownership. The result was a very successful year ... for all of us!

A Minor Shift in Objective Can Make a Big Difference

To expand its production capabilities, a U.S. manufacturer of ophthalmic lenses used in cataract surgery needed to transfer its technology for building the devices from its U.S. division to its European division.

We were brought in to work with the team and the transition. We were making excellent progress until we asked the team to clarify their objective. At that point, there was a discernible shift. The energy went from high to zero within a matter of minutes.

Sensing something wrong, I asked, "Is there something about this objective that isn't clear or that some people don't like? What's going on? What's the skunk under the table, the odor nobody is mentioning?"

After a couple of minutes, a few people from the U.S. division opened up. *Transferring* manufacturing knowledge and capability to Europe implied that the U.S. facility could potentially be closed – 600 American employees might eventually lose their jobs.

However unlikely it was, the possibility existed and there were some people at the U.S. plant who were concerned. No wonder the energy disappeared! Who would enthusiastically pursue an objective that could cost them their job?

When I asked senior management if their intention was to eventually lay off the American workers, their immediate response was "No, not at all!"

It wasn't about taking jobs from one plant and giving them to another. It was about expansion.

In this high-growth market for their product, the company needed additional manufacturing capacity – two factories instead of one. What came to light was that this was not really a team to transfer jobs and technology – it was a team to expand jobs and technology.

The sense of relief was significant. The misunderstanding that had surfaced through the right questions was resolved and the true objective was clarified.

The result? A high buy-in for the real goal.

Clarifying goals with Effective Questions – Step 3 of the Framework – offers an opportunity to make sure everyone is on the right track. Having unleashed your people's energy and creativity with Steps 1 and 2, you now harness that energy and creativity and direct them toward accomplishing clear and specific goals.

Once you generate enthusiasm and buy-in for the goal, the journey ahead will require less time and less wasted effort.

Of course, it's not always possible to achieve buy-in by allowing people to establish their own objectives. Sometimes the objective is passed down from above, or you are so clear about the objective, you're not open to discussing options.

In that case, you'll need to find alternate routes to buy-in. We'll address that in the next chapter.

Are you involved in a project that's off track? Can it benefit from having the stakeholders re-clarify the objective?

"Our life is frittered away by detail ...
Simplify, simplify."
– Henry David Thoreau

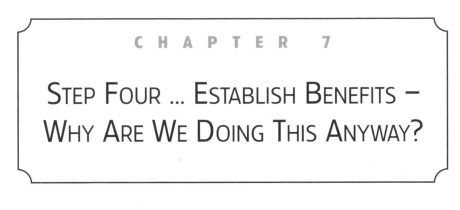

CHAPTER 7

STEP FOUR ... ESTABLISH BENEFITS – WHY ARE WE DOING THIS ANYWAY?

"The first and most important step toward success
is the feeling that we can succeed."
– Nelson Boswell

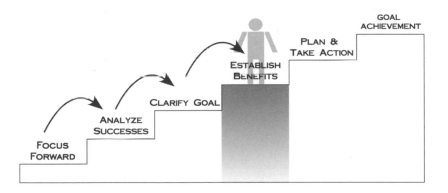

Key Question: *"What are the benefits of accomplishing our objective?"*

Step 4 of the Framework for Leadership encourages commitment to, and ownership of, the goal by those critical to implementing it.

When benefits for accomplishing the goal are clear for all stakeholders, including the department, the team and other individuals involved, buy-in is high and success is optimized.

By asking, "What are the benefits of accomplishing our objective?" the fourth step of the Framework seeks to uncover everyone's incentives, or lack of incentives, for achieving a goal.

When individuals find positive answers to the question, they acquire a personal stake in the outcome and will gladly focus energy, attention and resources on the tasks at hand. Without a clear, concrete stake in the outcome, however, motivation will vary based on each person's "accidental clarity" – his or her innate ability to sense why the mission is important.

> When people respond to the "benefits" question, they reveal their true reasons for investing in the goal, their underlying motivations.

Clear, intelligible answers to the Step 4 question establish a personal as well as a team buy-in.

When people respond to the "benefits" question, they reveal their true reasons for investing in the goal, their underlying motivations. By so doing, they will either validate or invalidate the objective as being worthy of their time and resources.

Every person who recognizes the project's benefits lends credibility to its accomplishment. Every individual's buy-in enhances the project's significance and validity, plus providing the greatest possibility for excellent results.

A clear example arose in our own company. For years, we promoted and delivered a public seminar in cities across the U.S. every month.

It was expensive to market and deliver these seminars, with most of the expenses occurring before the events took place.

We were averaging only 34 percent in upfront collections of fees. The result – we had a *big* cash-flow problem.

The manager of our public seminar department and our president facilitated a meeting. Using the Framework for Leadership, they focused on solving the problem … which was improving our collections to 75-80 percent.

When the "clarify the goal" step was reached, they asked, "What do you think you could accomplish if you really put your mind to it? What goal might you be able to achieve in terms of increasing the percentage of upfront collections?"

Immediately, one person asked, "If we really make a big improvement, how might we get rewarded?"

Realizing this would help the company significantly, the president said we would pay a bonus if the numbers were really good.

Knowing there was a payoff for them, our employees huddled in the conference room to come up with their own goal. When they were ready, they brought the two managers back inside.

"We think we can do 90 percent upfront collections!"

The senior managers were stunned and told them achieving that number would earn a significant bonus – and even specified what the bonus would be.

The employees were delighted to accept the challenge, though the managers weren't very optimistic.

Within two months, they were averaging 95 percent upfront collections, which was unheard of in the public seminar business! The company was much healthier, and the registration team was jubilant. The team had renewed focus and vision. The organization improved cash flow and the individuals received bonuses. Everyone won!

Costs vs. Benefits

The question, "Why are we doing this anyway?" prompts every stakeholder to run a cost-benefit analysis – if only in their head.

In doing so, each stakeholder will gauge: (A) if the goal offers any worthwhile personal benefits, and (B) whether the overall mission is likely to succeed.

Suppose you've just facilitated the planning process for a major project that will take a lot of time, money, resources and effort.

The group is clear on the objective. Now you ask the question, "What are the benefits for the customer, the company, this division, this team and each of you as individuals?"

Suppose there aren't a lot of benefits, or the benefits do not clearly offset the effort and investment required.

Realistically, you'd better take a serious look at this project. Why? Because it might not be worth doing!

Put simply, if people can't think of clear benefits for their efforts, then the goal, or how it is understood, needs to be revisited.

Harnessing Different Motivations

One advantage of this process: It clarifies and quantifies the benefits to everyone. It forces you to redefine the abstract as the concrete, leaving no room for vague or fuzzy promises.

Of course, you may have to dig deeper to unearth everyone's true motivations, but in many cases, repeating Step 4 – "What's the value/benefit of that?" – is sufficient. When someone says, "If this works, it would be fun," we ask something like, "What's the value to you, *personally?*"

This prompts people to reveal what's important to them at a deeper level. Or you might simply ask, "How would you quantify that benefit?"

The answer will tell you what's most important to that team member because each person may have entirely different motivations. Does one person want to know about return on investment? Is another concerned about the consequences to the organization's people? Someone might care most about an initiative's effect on customers, while another wants to know how it fits into the corporate culture.

Buy-in From All Stakeholders

Many times your team will have to get buy-in from upper management. The same benefit process applies ... what is the benefit to customers, shareholders, strategic partners, departments, vendors, etc.?

Before posing the Step 4 EQ "What are the benefits of accomplishing our objective?" to upper management, it makes sense to *first* pose the question on behalf of the other stakeholders.

In our experience, we find such discussions are most effective when they move from the

> ... Benefit discussions are most effective when they move from the "outside" to the "inside."

"outside" to the "inside." In other words, we first lead a discussion of how the project will benefit customers — those most outside the organization. Second, we address the benefits to shareholders or employees throughout the organization. And third, we discuss the department and team members most directly involved in implementing the program.

Because the "outside-in" approach demonstrates that many stakeholders will gain value from the project. It also serves as a reminder that it's permissible for us, as individuals, to feel we deserve some benefits, too.

Asking a subordinate, "What is the benefit for you, personally?" too soon might produce hesitation and concern, because he may not want to appear "selfish." But when it becomes clear that so many different stakeholders will benefit from the project, you're likely to receive honest answers from your team members, which will lead to a highly motivated team.

Perhaps a more effective way of asking the question to individuals is, "What will it do for you, personally?"

A good example of the true power of buy-in involved an information technology project at a major insurance company. The project manager had done everything he knew to get everyone focused on completing the project within the 30-day deadline, but it soon became clear, they wouldn't come close to meeting that target.

I brought the team together to introduce the Framework for Leadership and how it fit into the context of their project. The project manager then facilitated the Framework to create clear action plans for completing the project on time.

The first two steps went reasonably well. He captured numerous successes, as well as who and what contributed to those successes.

When he got to Step 3, "What is the objective?" the goal seemed clear, but I noticed a strange quiet in the room, almost lackadaisical.

Unsure of what to do about it, the project manager proceeded to Step 4, "What are the benefits of accomplishing the objectives – to the outside customers, the shareholders, the company, the division, the team, each of us as individuals?"

The feeling in the room was subdued as people shared typical reasons they felt the various stakeholders would benefit and how they would each, personally, benefit from finishing on time, but something was missing, and everyone knew it.

There was a skunk under the table that wasn't being identified.

Finally, out of frustration, the project manager blurted out, "... and you get to keep your jobs!"

People chuckled at first, but then they realized he was serious.

"What is that supposed to mean?" someone asked.

"I shouldn't have said that," the manager said quietly, "but rumor has it we are being watched very closely on this project, and if we don't finish on time, our roles could be outsourced to another company."

The room was stunned at this announcement and as discussions continued, the group soon realized no one had even thought the deadline was serious.

There had been no buy-in for the deadline and this new information – the possibility of being outsourced – fueled a completely new focus by the entire team.

Suddenly, there was 100 percent focus on what it would take to finish the project on time. Failure was no longer an option.

That's the real power of buy-in.

As for the rest of the story … they finished the project within the deadline – a small miracle.

We have the opportunity to gain the power of buy-in and ownership when we ask Step 4 questions like:

What are the benefits of accomplishing our objective?

What is the value for the company?

What will it do for you, personally?

What are some of the hidden benefits that might not be so obvious?

Now that we have strong ownership for the objective, we move to Step 5, the action-planning phase of the Framework.

STEP FIVE ... PLAN AND TAKE ACTION – THE SOLUTION STEP

"Even if you're on the right track,
you'll get run over if you just sit there."
– Will Rogers

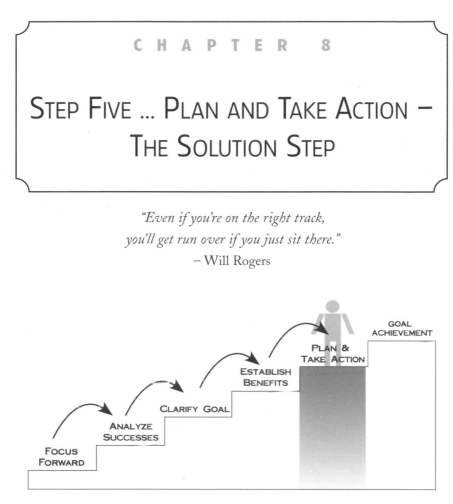

Key Question: What can we do more, better or differently to move closer to our objective?

Step 5 begins putting the solution into action.

All the previous steps of the process have been to prepare us for this step ... and, frankly, if we could go straight to this step and generate sufficient creativity, trust and openness, we would! However, experience has shown us if we move directly into brainstorming and problem-solving, the process doesn't often work.

> To reap the harvest, we must first prepare the soil and plant the seeds ... and the first two steps represent preparation and planting.

To reap the harvest, we must first prepare the soil and plant the seeds ... and the first two steps represent preparation and planting. Another part of the preparation is clarifying the objective – Step 3 – and developing the ownership, Step 4.

Step 5, the action plan, marks the beginning of the harvest and uses the creativity and enthusiasm generated through the first four steps to solve the problem.

The EQ, "What can we do more, better or differently to move closer to our objective?" gets everyone involved in the solution. It invites them to assume personal leadership and be part of the solution, not just part of the problem.

It also encourages people to share their ideas, knowledge and creativity ... and it honors their contributions.

The action plan establishes a true team approach to meeting the challenge. Everyone is encouraged to participate, and as they do, they almost always develop more effective solutions.

As they look at what can be done better or differently, notice they also are identifying what needs to change – a more palatable, less threatening way of looking at the problem. Then, as the action plan evolves, it moves them toward specific tasks and appropriate accountability.

Dave Malenfant, global supply-chain vice president for a worldwide company headquartered in Texas, had a problem: Product lead times in Europe were unacceptable. For months, his team had addressed this challenge without much improvement.

Having been introduced to the Framework for Leadership, Dave decided to meet with the European managers in Belgium, where he would use the process to address the issue.

Since the Framework was new to them, it wasn't surprising the European team started slowly. Each individual was trying to determine their role and gauge whether it was safe to contribute.

However, by the time they reached Step 5, the action step of the Framework, the room was charged with energy and creativity. Participation was at a high level, even though team members were impatient to "get to the solution."

Dave knew, at this point, it was extremely important to lay the groundwork before tackling the situation head-on. He knew the value of acknowledging the team for their successes and achievements before he invited them to do even better.

As soon as he asked the question, "What can we do more, better or differently to move closer to our objective?" one manager proposed a simple, yet brilliant, solution to the problem. It involved a clever way to reprioritize the order-taking process.

This one idea alone, which never came up during the previous months of traditional problem-solving and brainstorming, saved 20 days of lead time for the European operations.

The key to eliciting that elegant solution was to go through *all* the steps and gain the benefits of each. The process developed creative energy, trust and an openness resulting in ideas for solutions across the multinational organization.

A Continuous Process of Improvement

It may be neither realistic nor necessary to solve the entire problem in one huge bite, so the important part is just getting started toward a solution. By progressively biting off chewable chunks of the problem, the group will be better able to deal with them.

When we approach challenges using this method, we ensure our people won't be overwhelmed by large or difficult issues.

An insurance regional operations center was operating at a customer service rating of 58 percent, and achieving a rating anywhere near 90 percent seemed impossible. So, when management reached Step 3 of the Framework, "What are we trying to accomplish?" they knew not to set a huge numerical goal.

Instead, they let their people set the goal. When the claim center team established a goal of optimizing their customer service rating, they realized this would require an ongoing improvement process, and impressive numbers would not be created overnight.

The various teams started their periodic progress review meetings by celebrating the successes they'd had in customer service improvement since the last meeting (Step 1) and pinpointing what had contributed to those successes (Step 2).

Then, they asked, "What could we do more, better or differently to continue improving our level of customer service, thus increasing our approval rating?"

Each meeting provided ideas for improvement, some big and some small. When they were implemented, all of these ideas contributed to a customer service rating of 93 percent in 18 months!

While that represented, on average, less than two percent improvement each month, the continuous process of asking the right questions inspired everyone to keep going until they had the second best ratings in their Fortune 500 company.

They also reduced customer "hold time" from 20 minutes to under 20 seconds.

The purpose of the entire Framework is to create individual and group commitment to an effective action plan. The results achieved depend on the quality of the plan and the degree of ownership (commitment) to implementing it.

As individual team members get involved in the solution steps, the process reaffirms their commitment to results. Soon, they are, naturally, going to be highly committed to the ideas they have contributed.

Results = Quality of Plan x Degree of Buy-in: A great plan with poor buy-in yields poor results. A mediocre plan with high buy-in yields good results. When the Framework for Leadership is used, the plan improves significantly, due to the benefits derived from the Forward Focus perspective. People work harder and smarter to create a quality plan, and their ownership builds during the process. The results are excellent and, many times, even extraordinary.

> As individual team members get involved in the solution steps, the process reaffirms their commitment to results.

Accountability: There is a second, critically important part to Step 5. The responses to this question determine who will be responsible for specific tasks. Therefore, it is imperative for everyone to be clear about their specific role and the expectations established for that role. The basic question is: *Who will do what by when?*

> Good plans aren't useful unless someone is accountable for implementing them.

Good plans aren't useful unless someone is accountable for implementing them. We remember the first time we used this accountability question, "Who will do what by when?" in our own company's strategic planning process.

We were curious to see people's responses because now we were asking them to take responsibility for action. Would they really want to do the work?

They enjoyed the creative process, but would they actually sign up for the activities required to accomplish the results we wanted? As it turned out, any questions or concerns we might have had were unjustified. When people are creatively involved in planning the solutions, they are eager to participate in the implementation!

People volunteered to do things we didn't even know they could do.

Do people have "glass ceilings?" You bet! However, by asking, "Who is willing or would like to do this?" you can remove, or at least raise, those ceilings as people step up to the need. Remember, however, they aren't likely to volunteer for things for which they have no capacity.

Ed's older daughter, Robin, was a college student who managed to squeeze four years of college into five years. (Yes, she approved this comment.) So, when Robin came to work at Enlightened Leadership, while she continued to "look for a real job," Ed wasn't expecting her to contribute a great deal. Imagine his proud surprise when Robin was quick to respond with an enthusiastic, "I'll do that!" when the team was asked "Who will do what by when?"

Caution: The initial action plan does not need to fully accomplish the objective. Because the ultimate goal may be too large or complex, you should not expect a comprehensive plan to evolve overnight. There is little value in putting undue pressure on yourself and your team to develop all the answers at once. The initial plan might simply involve some research, discussing the scope with stakeholders, or experimenting with a specific approach. Too much pressure could actually stifle the creative process – and it is a *process*.

Keep in mind that it's far more important to generate an interim action plan that gets you moving *toward* a solution.

Step 5 is the *beginning* of the action plan. You will have plenty of opportunities to fill in more of the pieces that contribute to the final solution as you move along.

The Solution Might Come Quickly

On the other hand, be open to the possibility of "miracle" solutions … brilliant ideas that are easy to implement and achieve major results quickly.

Penny's Disease Control Team, mentioned in an earlier chapter, quickly developed breakthrough ideas about how to provide lower costs while maintaining isolated housing for tuberculosis patients. This happened almost immediately after the team shifted from a problem-orientation to a solution-orientation.

That shift happened easily and early in the five-step Framework process. Those initial solutions continue to save the county approximately $250,000 every quarter while providing a higher quality of living for the patients.

Measuring Progress

There is one more important aspect of Step 5 – how to evaluate progress.

While you could establish measurement criteria in the goal-setting of Step 3, it would tend to limit your options for solutions. By waiting until you have brainstormed ways to reach your objective before establishing measurement criteria, your team is allowed to think outside the box about solutions.

Once solution ideas are in hand, deciding how to measure progress creates additional clarity about the goal. The basic question is:

How will we measure progress?

It Does Not Take Experts to Facilitate

When A.J. Hiltenbrand facilitated the workshop for dozens of people from several countries, his role was to provide some context for the work, teach the 40-plus people how to utilize the Framework and then step back and watch them do it.

While he remained available for support, the primary facilitation was actually done by the participants, divided into logical, functional groups of four to six people.

Some parts of the facilitation went more smoothly than others, yet they all produced substantial results.

They proved you do not have to be a trained facilitator to use this tool. In fact, so many cost savings and additional profits were uncovered in that one meeting, the participants immediately committed to holding another session the following year for four more European countries.

When we ask the Step 5 Effective Questions, the value of the Framework for Leadership comes together as the Action Plan and the assigned responsibilities for the solution are determined.

The basic questions are:

> *What can we do more, better or differently to move closer to our objective?*
>
> *Who will do what by when?*
>
> *and How will we measure progress?*

All five steps of the Framework for Leadership have been presented. The next chapter brings all five steps together and looks at the entire process.

PULLING IT ALL TOGETHER – GOAL ACHIEVEMENT

"Coming together is a beginning; keeping together is progress; working together is success."

– Henry Ford

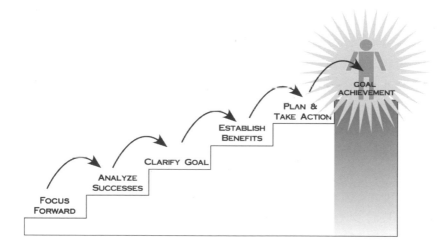

Now, let's put together all five steps of the Framework for Leadership:

Step 1. What is already working?

Step 2. What makes it work?

Step 3. What are we trying to accomplish?

Step 4. What are the benefits of achieving the objective?

Step 5. What can we do more, better or differently to move closer to the objective?

Let's review all five steps to see how they fit together.

1. **"What is already working?** What successes have we had? What is working well? What are you pleased about?"

   These types of questions prime the pump of creativity and become solution-focused. The responses develop positive energy and enthusiasm. Because the questions focus on what is working, they tend to be safe to answer. This builds trust. When energy is high and trust is strong, creative problem-solving is unleashed.

2. **"What makes it work?** What caused that success? To what do you attribute that success? What about this success pleases you the most? What specific talents most contributed to the success?"

   These are questions organizations and people seldom ask, yet the costs of not asking them are substantial. When a team really understands the cause of a success, they can leverage that knowledge in other situations. Organizations tend to be quick to perform root-cause analysis of problems, yet they seldom do root-cause analysis of successes.

Asking, "What makes it work?" is energizing because it invites the acknowledgement of specific people as they are describing what they contributed to the success.

3. **"What are we trying to accomplish?"** or **"What is the objective?"**

Having built participation, acknowledgement and learning in the first two steps, this third step is an opportunity to look at the objectives to determine if they're the right ones ... and to see if everyone is on the same track. When the team members are involved in determining objectives, they are more likely to be accountable for achieving them.

4. **"What are the benefits of achieving the objective?** What will it do for each of the stakeholders?"

This is the buy-in step. When people are clear about what's in it for them, you can stand back and watch things happen. If stakeholders aren't clear about the personal benefits, good luck getting anything done, no matter what you do. This step is particularly important when launching a major project or initiating a turnaround or change, where substantial buy-in is needed from the start.

5. **"What can we do more, better or differently to move closer to the objective?** Who will do what by when? How will we measure progress?"

These questions take advantage of the creativity that's been generated and the clarity of the goal that's been established to determine the action plan, the individual tasks and the accountability for those tasks. The power in this step comes from the creative energy generated in the other steps. Again, you allow the complete action plan to naturally evolve over time.

Where Does the Problem Show Up?

Let's pause to ask a question about this process. Are we ignoring the problem? If not, where does the "problem" show up in the Framework?

You probably realized the "problem" is merely the gap between Step 1, "What is already working?" and Step 3, "What are we trying to accomplish?"

To solve the "problem," simply do what's necessary to close the gap.

Imagine starting a meeting by throwing the problem onto the conference room table. Can you sense people posturing to make sure they don't get blamed for the problem?

Now imagine using the entirely different approach of clarifying where you already are (What's working?), looking at where you want to go (What do we want to accomplish?), and realizing the challenge is to close the gap between the two.

> *No one* wants to be part of the problem, but *everyone* wants to be part of the solution.

The first approach creates defensiveness, and the second approach shifts people to a solution-orientation.

No one wants to be part of the problem, but *everyone* wants to be part of the solution. That bears repeating: No one really wants to be part of the problem … but everyone wants to be part of the solution.

Circle of Transformation™

By using the Framework for Leadership as a continuous process, the possibility of breakthrough ideas – or transformation – is enhanced.

Since Step 5 is the action plan, the next step would be the implementation. Once the plan is being implemented, it is important to monitor and communicate progress continually.

♦ To do that, start with Step 1 again, "What is working so far?" Celebrating the early successes opens creativity for the next steps and keeps the focus on the next level of solution.

♦ Analyzing those successes in Step 2, "What is causing those successes?" adds more enthusiasm and creativity to the process.

♦ Checking in on Step 3, "What are we trying to accomplish?" might determine the goal has not changed. However, as this circular process continues through multiple cycles, there may be a time when a realization occurs that the "real" goal is something else. When that happens, the new clarity is virtually always inspiring.

♦ If the goal has not changed, there might be little need to review Step 4, "What are the benefits for all the stakeholders?"

♦ Step 5 is nearly always critical, "What else can we do to move closer to the goal?"

The following graphic illustrates the circular nature of practicing the Framework for Leadership. This continuous improvement version is called the Circle of Transformation™.

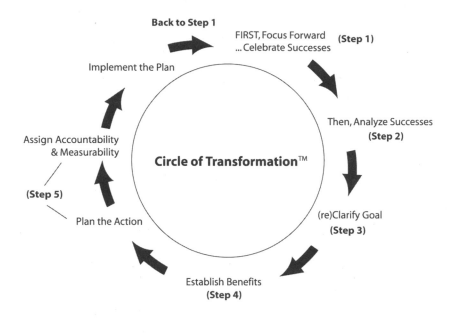

"Winning organizations not only fulfill their desired goals today, but they also continually redesign those goals as circumstances change and go on to meet those new goals."

– Noel Tichy

CHAPTER 1 0

EXAMPLES OF THE FRAMEWORK FOR LEADERSHIP IN ACTION

Planning and Implementation

Tony Lynn, the founder and owner of a mid-size leather importer, invited team members to his house one Saturday. His intent was to use the Framework for Leadership process to do some planning for the next year.

Since he'd never taken this particular approach, he wasn't sure what would happen, but he courageously launched into the process. Right away, people started sharing successes.

Enthusiasm grew … and while it was very positive and energizing for the group, there were no real surprises until he reached Step 3 and asked, "What objectives do you want to have for next year that would really motivate you?"

Tony was surprised when the team established some lofty goals – ones he wasn't sure they could accomplish. One goal seemed especially impossible: moving out of their warehouse and office (with two more years on the existing lease) and into a better, larger space.

Tony didn't think such an envisioned space even existed in the area. He certainly didn't think moving was possible – given the lease situation.

Immediately after this goal-clarifying meeting, Tony's team began working diligently on the projects and used the Framework EQs to review and to keep the team progressing.

They stayed focused and enthusiastic as they experienced success after success, energized further by celebrating each of them.

All of this occurred with very little help from Tony, who was traveling extensively.

Therefore, he was most enthusiastic of all when the team accomplished several annual goals within six months, including moving into a beautiful new office and warehouse space.

Tony's team had, seemingly, done the impossible. The ideas and enthusiasm generated at Tony's house that Saturday had begun a positive contagion of actions, leading to results.

Managing Cross-functional Project Teams

Rancho Cordova had sought to become its own city – without success – on more than one occasion. With a vision and focus on the future, the board of directors of the Rancho Cordova Chamber of Commerce engaged its members and energized the community for another try.

Lee Casaleggio was asked to facilitate the board's two-year planning meeting that preceded the incorporation election. In a fairly conventional but energetic two-day retreat, the board worked long hours to create the blueprint of activities and accountabilities needed for success.

Six months later, after Lee had been through an Enlightened Leadership Train-the-Facilitator course, he met with the board again to assess progress on the plan, which had some significant issues.

Lee proposed using the Framework for Leadership, explaining it as a different way of approaching this type of meeting. Reaction was immediate:

"Aren't we going to discuss the problems we're having?"

"No," Lee said.

"What!!?" was the incredulous reply.

Lee asked for their trust and received a grudging go-ahead.

With the first question – "In implementing our plan, where have we been successful?" – examples exploded from members. They interrupted each other to share achievements.

At the end of the discussion, the group had filled all 16 flip charts, hung around the room.

With the second question, "What has caused these successes?" the group turned quietly analytical, but not for long. The energy behind the cause-and-effect responses mirrored the success stories.

As they filled the flip charts, a trend appeared – the name of the Chamber's Executive Director appeared as a primary cause for success on 14 of the sheets.

"I get it!" came the cry from the member who had asked if they were going to discuss problems. "In all our previous meetings, we pummeled our director for all the things that hadn't been done. Clearly, from what we see on our walls, we've spread the director too thin. Obviously, we've got to get more of us involved."

At this point, Lee is fond of recalling, there was a tear on the director's cheek. His need for more help had always been there. It was simply invisible from the focus on problems.

Questions 3 and 4 were swiftly and joyfully completed – the group was committed to incorporation, and they were passionate and clear about the benefits to the community.

> The Framework for Leadership became a framework for success.

The Step 5 question, "What do we need to do more, better or differently?" was answered by rapid volunteering for support assignments and delegation of tasks. The Framework for Leadership became a framework for *success*, *beginning* with the citizens' vote of approval on Nov. 5, 2002, and, ultimately, the incorporation of the City of Rancho Cordova on July 1, 2003.

Getting Buy-In for Change

A division of a major pharmaceutical company was making a change in compensation for its manufacturing workers. Sharon, a key department manager, knew this change represented a big challenge.

Having been introduced to the Framework shortly before, she decided to facilitate a discussion about the new compensation plan ... and because she didn't know of a better approach, the risk didn't seem too high.

Using the Framework, she asked people which aspects of the new compensation program they liked. Then she asked what they liked, specifically.

She then asked plenty of "What else?" questions, and then reviewed the new plan's objectives, which had been set by corporate.

Next, she facilitated a discussion about the benefits of achieving those objectives – for the customer, the company, the division, the team and for each employee individually.

Finally, Sharon asked her co-workers to look at how the plan met these objectives, inviting them to propose ways to make it better – with the proviso she didn't have the last word on those decisions.

By the end of the process, Sharon was delighted to find she'd achieved a good level of buy-in for the new plan, which had rarely happened in the past.

Employee skepticism was minimal and they acknowledged her for having facilitated an open discussion about the compensation plan.

Sharon, in turn, credited the Forward Focused approach of the Framework for the success. During the process, the workers also came up with a few ideas for improving the system, some of which Sharon was able to implement.

Creating Visions or Ideal Models

One of the Framework's greatest strengths is developing collaborative visions or ideal models. The third step, "What are we trying to accomplish?" becomes "What is our ideal model or vision of what we want to do?"

Be forewarned, however, that sometimes, we take our work home with us. When Jonette and Ed first became engaged, we wanted to create our ideal relationship vision. Since we knew the Framework was just the ticket for doing this, we planned an entire evening at a quiet, romantic restaurant – with pads of paper and pens in hand.

After ordering dinner, we began with "What do we already appreciate about each other or our relationship?" We took turns sharing, and of course, kept asking, "What else?" When something shared was more of a surface factor, we would ask the other person to go deeper with precisely what they appreciated and why (Step 2). Jonette and I filled up several sheets with responses from the first two steps.

It was a great way to spend an evening (in mutual admiration), so we were in no hurry to finish.

When we had exhausted ideas for Steps 1 and 2, we moved to the final step – Step 3, "What is our ideal relationship vision?"

As soon as we asked that question, we realized we already knew! It was everything we already appreciated about our relationship. We just needed to simplify the vision, using all of our notes.

Furthermore, this was an opportunity to look at aspects of our ideal vision that might, currently, not be strong in the relationship.

This last step was the most challenging because it represented gaps and issues in our current relationship.

The deep sharing of appreciation in the first two steps, though, had opened our hearts and prepared us for a new level of openness and honesty.

The resulting "Jonette's Relationship Vision" was calligraphed, framed and hung in our bedroom … and every now and then, it serves as a tool to remind us of our shared vision!

Conflict Resolution

Susan Dixon, an assistant principal, needed to deal with a sensitive situation involving two co-teachers. Although the two had been good friends, their relationship had deteriorated and was beginning to impact the quality of their teaching. Now, parents were beginning to show their concern.

Dixon had scheduled a meeting with the quarreling teachers, and having been introduced to the Framework fairly recently, she thought it might have a chance of working – at least better than any of the other ideas she had!

The assistant principal set the tone for the meeting by sharing she had some concerns about the teachers' relationship and how it was affecting the students.

She then suggested she wanted to facilitate a specific discussion and, after reminding the teachers they had been good friends, the assistant principal jumped into the process by asking, "What are some of the things each of you appreciate about the other?"

There was a long silence before one teacher acknowledged the other for something she appreciated. The other teacher was then motivated to share something good about her co-worker.

A series of "what else?" questions was key here. As they loosened up, the comments and responses got stronger and deeper as they gradually shifted their mindset back to what they really appreciated about each other.

Occasionally, Susan – the facilitator – would say, "Say more about that" or something similar to encourage depth and sincerity.

By this time, the statements were all quite positive, and the co-workers were remembering what they had appreciated about each other all along. Because of a recent conflict, which did not need to be discussed at all, they had been distracted and had lost focus of the more important aspects of their relationship.

Now that they were back on track, Susan asked, "What is your common goal here?" (Step 3)

It only took a split second for both of them to jump in and confirm the goal was, indeed, to provide the best possible education for their students.

"Well, you certainly have the right goal," Susan affirmed. "What are some things each of you can do to make sure you're accomplishing that goal?"

As the teachers responded, there was a new level of energy, enthusiasm and focus and, by the end of the session, they were back in a friendly relationship and moving forward, together, again.

Running Forums with Multiple Stakeholders

Cathy Singletary, a division manager in a major Social Services agency's Children's Services Division, uses the Framework in many different ways – training, best practices, quality assurance, legislative implementation, development of policy & procedure, etc.

The application she likes best, however, involves community forums when she goes to the community for their input on Child Welfare's Strategic Plan.

When the forums were just beginning, Cathy's director wouldn't let her use the Framework in the community groups because he felt it was too risky. Essentially, the meetings were full of dissension and disagreement.

Then, quite unexpectedly, her director gave the go-ahead because, as he put it, "It couldn't be any worse than what they already tried!"

Use of the 5 steps of the Framework was overwhelmingly successful and resulted in a strategic plan with strong community buy-in. Why? Because the community stakeholders felt heard and became a part of the solution.

Now, as a result, the Framework is just the way they do business as well as a valuable, continuous quality-improvement tool.

Sometimes It Can Be Even Simpler!

The five-step Framework for Leadership is a simple approach to collaboratively deal with your greatest management challenges, yet sometimes you don't need every step.

We've included some examples of how you can "tailor" or "personalize" the Framework to fit any situation.

The "mini" Framework

One manager wanted those reporting to him to evaluate his performance, so he called a meeting and invited them to answer two questions. The first was a typical, positive, or Forward Focused question he could pose in a number of ways: "What do you appreciate about how I work with you?" Or, "What am I doing well in my role?"

Traditionally, the next question would be the challenging one – the "What's wrong?" question, or "What needs improvement?" or "What do you see as my issue?" or "What do I do poorly?"

No matter how it's worded, the follow-up question is sometimes more challenging because it can create defensiveness. In the best case, the question might be phrased as, "Where do I need improvement?"

However, in the case of our manager who had been taught the Framework for Leadership, his second question was a little different … "What would you like to see me do *even better* than I'm already doing?"

Think about that question. What is the implication? Well, it implies the manager was already doing well, *to some degree*, in most everything he was doing – which was true. (And that's probably true for almost everyone.)

Notice: There is nothing to get defensive about. Everyone can always do *even better*, whatever his or her current level of performance.

In our experience, there is something magical in the "even better" terminology.

The first time the manager facilitated this process, he was overwhelmed with the value and quality of his employees' feedback. With that second question, there were no "need to's" or "should's" about his performance. There was no sense of judgment … only comments such as, "I would like to see you acknowledge me when I do good work more often than you already do."

> The quality of the response is directly related to the quality of the question.

How could you get defensive over that type of feedback? **Notice:** the quality of the response is directly related to the quality of the question.

Because of the way the feedback was given, the manager could really hear it, and the people felt listened to. It was such an open and powerful experience for him, the manager has encouraged managers in every department of his company to try it for themselves.

The key to the success of the process was that both questions were Forward Focused. There was no "What's wrong?" question to create defensiveness.

The generic **mini-Framework** often looks like this:

1. What are we already doing well?

2. What could we do even better?

These are, simply, Steps 1 and 5 of the Framework for Leadership.

It's Your Ship

In his best-selling book, *It's Your Ship: Management Techniques From the Best Damn Ship in the Navy*, Commander Mike Abrashoff reported using his own version of a mini-Framework when he asked each of his crew on the *USS Benfold* the following three questions:

1. What do you like most about your experience on the *USS Benfold*?

2. What do you like least about your experience on the *Benfold*?

3. What would you change if you could?

All three questions are Forward Focused, including the second one. Note the difference between "What do you like least?" vs. "What do you NOT like?"

What do you think would happen if the sailors onboard the *Benfold* had been asked, "What don't you like about your experience on the *Benfold*?"

Responses would probably have been something like, "Nothing, sir! I like everything, sir!" But truthfully, everyone has *something* he or she likes the "least." So the question is not threatening when worded, "What do you like least?"

This is just one example of a subtle change that makes a profound difference.

As a result, Commander Abrashoff got honest, useful answers.

By the time the interviews were finished, he knew exactly what was working well on the *Benfold* and what needed attention. The interview process had a great impact on his priorities for turning around the poorly performing ship and dramatically improving morale.

Three of the many impressive results included:

1) Becoming the top performing ship in the history of the Pacific fleet,

2) Retaining 100% of its crew,

3) Returning nearly 20% of its budget to Navy coffers.

Mike Abrashoff had not read our book, nor had he participated in any of our workshops. His own quest to be a more effective leader led him to discover these simple tools for himself.

When Time is Limited ...

Many opportunities arise during the day to incorporate the essence of the Framework by helping people feel acknowledged and getting them focused on what's important.

Think of all those hallway or water-cooler conversations that might utilize simple Step 1 and 5 questions like:

What are you feeling good about? What successes are you having? What else?

What, specifically, are you looking to improve over the next couple of weeks? What ideas do you have for doing that?

A conversation that includes these simple questions could last just a couple of minutes, or it could lead to additional discussions. Either way, there's always an opportunity to provide value by asking the right questions.

Audits Made Fun!

Audits – of any kind – provide the perfect environment where the "mini" Framework can make a difference.

If someone walked into your office and said, "The auditors are coming tomorrow morning," what would you think or feel?

The auditing group of a mid-size CPA firm knew their clients were seldom happy to see them. After experiencing the EQ process of the Framework, they immediately saw the possibility of changing the negative image of auditors and the auditing process.

"Wow! It sure would be different if our clients felt our intention was to document and share all the ways they were *already* being effective and how they could be even better," one auditor pointed out. "They might even look forward to our audits!"

"That might be a bit exaggerated," laughed a colleague, "but it sure would make the whole process a more positive experience for them … and us, too."

They left the session that day committed to changing the relationship with their auditing clients.

Imagine if all auditors shifted to this, "What is working?" and "What could work even better?" mindset with the idea of doing a "successful practice" audit!

Perhaps you really would look forward to the arrival of the auditors!

When You Are Clear about Objectives and Benefits …

Another opportunity to simplify the Framework process is when you are in the middle of a project and you're clear about its objectives and the benefits. You don't need to review them every time you meet. Periodically, however, there might be value in verifying that your goals haven't changed, but not every time.

For example, if you had a meeting last week that resulted in a very clear objective for your team's project, you can skip Step 3, "What is our objective?" when you have your next meeting or project review.

To promote continuous improvement, using the Effective Question process of the Framework, you only need to ask:

1. What is already working?

2. What could we/you do even better?

While these questions are usually quite powerful, there are certain situations in which a completely Forward Focused approach might not work.

CHAPTER 12

EMOTIONS IN THE WORKPLACE – DEALING WITH REALITY

There is a time when Forward Focus and Effective Questions will not shift negative mindsets. You may have experienced such situations where you were discussing an idea, project or a change for which you wanted buy-in and commitment.

Perhaps everyone was quiet or some were nodding their heads in agreement, but the sense of commitment was not there. Something was missing. Something was not being said ... that smelly skunk under the table.

Some of the participants knew what it was, but no one was talking. You could only feel the fear and knew it was limiting people's ability to focus forward in any way.

The idea of Forward Focus won't work when someone is afraid or so stuck in negative emotions they can't shift.

So, what's your next step?

The best way to deal with those concerns is to put them on the table so they can be discussed and defused.

A simple way to start the process is to ask:

What concerns do you have?

The Ultimate BACKWARD Focus

Fear is the ultimate *backward* focus. It paralyzes us into thinking only the worst can happen, so we're prevented from consciously choosing to Focus Forward.

An example of a team holding back because of concerns occurred on a recent trek on Mt. Kilimanjaro in East Africa. Our team was quieter than usual while having pre-dinner tea at the 15,000-ft. summit base camp. Ralph Johnson, our Swedish friend, was particularly quiet, which was unlike him under normal conditions. I felt that any attempted discussion would be superficial unless the hidden issue was uncovered and diffused.

I asked Ralph if it was okay to ask him a direct question. Getting his permission, I asked, "What concerns do you have about what happened on the trail today?" Although silent until then, Ralph quickly indicated that some feelings might have been hurt when some of us broke away from the slower group to reach camp sooner. Five or six people then contributed to a great conversation about the situation, sharing different perspectives. That got the team past the concerns, and allowed us to refocus on the major challenge of climbing the mountain. It was a critical moment for our team. Ralph expressed appreciation for the question and acknowledged the value of the team discussion.

Miraculous Facilitation

Negative emotions can paralyze your team.

Carol Bergmann, author of *Managing Your Energy at Work*, was a regional quality manager for a large professional software services firm and was often called in to support different management teams and groups across the country.

At one point, she was asked to work with an office having major issues.

After some investigation, Carol found the management team had done a good job of meeting with employees and listening to the issues, yet they couldn't come up with a solution. So, Carol, who had just been introduced to the Framework, decided to give it a try.

When she walked into the meeting room, Carol said she could have cut the negative atmosphere with a knife! It was uncomfortable for everyone – and very tense.

Given this environment, Carol made an excellent decision. She decided she could *not* start this meeting with "What is working?" because she felt the employees needed to vent their hostilities. Instead, she asked, "What is the situation you're dealing with? What's going on?" (That was her way of saying, "What concerns do you have?")

After that opening, Carol was flooded with issues of every shape and description. However, her approach immediately dissipated the negative energy and fears crowding into the room that day, which was exactly Carol's objective.

Only then were the participants ready to be Forward Focused.

With that preparation, Carol took a deep breath and asked, "I've heard a lot of the problems. Now tell me, what's *working* on this project? Since you've been at it for a year and a half, something must be working."

There was a long, uncomfortable silence and Carol allowed that silence as she waited patiently – an important aspect of facilitation.

Then, after what seemed like an eternity, one woman mentioned a report she had created for the group that was helpful to their communications.

More silence followed before another woman mentioned a tool she had developed that had been helpful to the team and the client.

Soon, descriptions of other successes came more and more rapidly and, by the end of the discussion, Carol had filled five flip charts with their successes on the project.

For each of those, she drilled deeper to capture the cause of the success or a better understanding of it (Step 2).

The positive energy was amazing! The entire atmosphere had completely, and dramatically, changed.

From there, Carol moved to Step 3, "What are you trying to accomplish?" With this question, she probed what the group *wanted* to accomplish and what they felt they *could* accomplish, given the limitations they were facing.

Establishing their goals clearly and positively, the group then discussed the benefits of accomplishing them as the energy remained high and positive, even increasing during the benefits discussion.

When they were ready for Step 5 – the Action Plan – Carol got out of the way and let the staff do the work. Their enthusiasm was impressive as they created their plans and strategies.

"They realized they had their own solutions all along," Carol pointed out, "but they had been waiting for management to solve their problems and tell them what to do."

The breakthrough that day was a miracle! And, bottom line, the only thing the group really needed from management was a pizza budget.

Two months later, Carol visited the group to check on their progress and found they were well along on implementing their plans. The group also was meeting frequently over pizza and using the Framework to continue the process they had started.

Most importantly, the project was back on track and the once damaged relationship with the client had been mended in a major way.

Sometimes, the most Effective Question you can ask is a question that allows people to share their concerns, their fears, or whatever is keeping them stagnated – before inviting them to Focus Forward again.

This modified process might look like:

What concerns do you have about this situation?

What's not being said?

What's going on?

What am I missing in this discussion?

What fears do you have about this?

What is the "elephant" in the room that is not being discussed?

CHAPTER 13

THE INTENTION BEHIND THE QUESTIONS

"Leadership is making the complex simple."
– Anonymous

In providing leadership that transformed the effectiveness of his destroyer-class naval vessel to attain the *highest* combat readiness in the history of the Pacific fleet, Commander Mike Abrashoff used the essence of this Framework.

Remember, Mike had never heard of Enlightened Leadership Solutions – the company or the book. He just did what worked!

He certainly didn't pace around the ship thinking, "Let's see, I should start this meeting with Step 1 of the Framework!" Instead, he naturally focused on the right things because that was what he needed to do to be effective … and so it is with the best leaders.

The Role of Intention

Think about the "intention" behind the questions you ask, or for that matter, the statements you make.

If you're really upset with someone who made a big mistake, if you ask, "What are you trying to accomplish?" – as innocent as that reads on paper – you may come across as very threatening.

Therefore, even more important than specific wording is your underlying agenda – or intention with the questions you ask and your timing in using them.

Taking this concept one step further, if you're upset about something, you cannot be emotionally Forward Focused at the same moment. It's impossible.

The people around you will sense you're upset and their fears will start to surface. When this happens, individual and team effectiveness is compromised … kaput!

So, in order to provide effective leadership, you must deal with your own emotions – whatever that takes – before you can get back to a productive intention. Otherwise, you are likely to react in an emotionally negative way and, in doing so, create additional problems.

The Intent of the Framework for Leadership

The intent of the Framework, as a whole, is to optimize the effectiveness with which an individual, team or organization achieves its mission, vision or goal.

Let's look at the intention behind each of the individual steps, or questions:

1. What is already working, or what successes are we having?
   The fundamental intention of this step is to shift individuals, groups or teams into being solution-focused (Forward Focused) rather than problem-focused. An additional intent is to build

creative energy within the individual or group. This will prepare them to resolve the issue or meet the challenge in later steps.

To accomplish these "hard" intents, a primary intent is to have the people involved feel honored for who they are and what they have already done, thus opening them to the possibility of what more they could be and achieve.

Without this underlying intention, the question doesn't work.

Without a doubt, the Step 1 question is a tool to build a high-performance environment, and it can be very effective … as long as it's backed by the right intention.

2. What made it work, or caused the success?

The underlying intention here is to learn from past successes so they can be repeated. Now, if the *real* intent is to find out what went wrong, who screwed up and the reason why, you'll never take this Forward Focused question seriously.

If everyone who read *Leadership Made Simple* were to make just this one change – to consistently look for and analyze successes – this book would make a significant difference.

Bottom line, it's a big opportunity for everyone who wants to provide leadership to become more effective … in a single step.

3. What are we trying to accomplish?

The intention of Step 3 is to get everyone on the *same* page and make sure it's the *right* page. Step 3 makes sure everyone is pulling in the same direction, thus maximizing the group's efforts. It's all about alignment.

This question also provides an opportunity to continually challenge the status quo – a key responsibility of leadership.

Situations change and this means our objectives might need to be revisited. Or, what is a higher-level goal that could be even more inspiring? Or, are the current objectives still appropriate? These are all important reflections – and the Step 3 question invites that reflection.

This goal-setting step also defines the gap between where you are and where you want to be. It sets up the problem that must be solved or the challenge that must be met – in a Forward Focused manner.

4. **What are the benefits – for each of the stakeholders – of achieving our objectives?**
   The intention here is determining whether everyone is clear and committed to the goal. When people know "what's in it for them," you don't need to worry about getting things done.

   When people are clear about their personal benefit, buy-in and motivation become high for achieving the objective. It's also an opportunity to make sure the benefits equal – or outweigh – the efforts needed to achieve the goal.

5. **What can we do more, better or differently to move closer to the objective? Who will do what by when? How will we measure progress?**
   This is where the "rubber meets the road." To this point, the entire Framework for Leadership is designed to prepare for this step – the Action Plan. The intention? To tap into the creativity unleashed from the positive environment established in the earlier steps.

This step represents a Forward Focused approach to dealing with obstacles, challenges, problems and issues. Remember, the problem is, simply, the gap between what's already working and what we want to accomplish.

These Step 5 questions are designed to generate the action plan and the accountability needed to close, or begin to close, that gap. Step-by-step implementation of that plan moves us closer and closer to the objective. Additionally, the plan also establishes how we will measure our success.

The Natural Leader

The leader "coming from" the true intent of the Framework for Leadership, then, is naturally and continually:

♦ Looking for successes to celebrate and opportunities to acknowledge people – just to let them know they are appreciated and to get them Forward Focused.

♦ Learning from those successes and encouraging others to do the same.

♦ Assuring team members or the individual are focused on the right objectives and equipped to challenge the status quo.

♦ Making sure everyone is clear about the personal benefits they will receive from being part of the solution, as well as understanding the benefits for all the stakeholders ... and knowing both these factors will dramatically impact the outcome.

♦ Developing increasingly better solutions by tapping into the enhanced creativity, enthusiasm and commitment developed with the other steps.

♦ Assuring accountability for the implementation of the plan.

♦ Assuring clarity on how to measure progress.

Again, the best leaders do this naturally. It is just who they *are*. They are not so much "doing" – they are "being." It's where they "come from."

The vast majority of us are in the process of "becoming" – becoming the best leaders we can be, the best person we can be, the best spouse, the best father or the best mother or friend.

For those of us who are "becoming," the Framework for Leadership is a powerful model and tool for achieving new levels of effectiveness and being.

By consciously using the essence of the Framework in what we do – with the right intentions behind our actions – we will be encouraged by the results we get – and our experiences from using the Framework will stimulate us to keep doing it.

> When people are immersed in an environment where the Framework for Leadership is being used, they will be motivated and inspired to be the best they can be.

Remember: The more we use the process, the better our results will be – and the more it will become part of who we are.

Not only are the results achieved with the Framework continuously improving and sometimes transformational, but the people around us will be transformed as well.

When people are immersed in an environment where the Framework for Leadership is being used, they will be motivated and inspired to be the best they can be.

You'll know this is working when they start running on the questions even before you ask them!

Indeed, not only are the people around you transformed, but the more you practice the essence of the Framework for Leadership, the more you *become* the essence of what it represents. The day you realize that you aren't thinking about Steps 1 through 5, but, instead, are just naturally behaving from the perspectives they represent, you'll know that you've been transformed.

A Personal Challenge

We'd like to end with a personal challenge.

♦ **Where could you use the essence of this Framework for Leadership in the next seven days that might make a difference?**

♦ **How could you use it for an important meeting, a project review, a conflict you must resolve, a performance review, launching a new initiative, or getting a team better aligned and focused?**

Whatever the need, we invite you to use it and e-mail us about your success at contactus@enleadership.com. If you do that, we believe the Framework for Leadership will be your "friend for life!"

QUESTIONS FOR SPECIFIC APPLICATIONS

Framework for Personal Conflict Resolution:

1. What are some things you appreciate about each other? What else?

2. What, specifically, do you appreciate about that?

3. What is your common goal or interest in this situation?

4. What would be the benefit for each of you to accomplish that?

5. What could each of you do to move closer to that goal? What else?

Framework for Win-Win Negotiation:

1. Where do we already agree? Where else?

2. What is it about those situations that cause us to agree?

3. What are the overall goals that are important to us?

4. How will we benefit from accomplishing those goals?

5. What one thing could either of us do right now to move closer to those goals? What else?

Framework for Individual Performance Improvement:

1. What are the areas of your performance about which you feel best? What are some of your successes? What else?

2. What personal strengths, specifically, support those successes? What else?

3. What are the most important objectives of your role?

4. What would be the benefits to the team when you accomplish those? To you personally?

5. What are some specific things you can do to come closer to meeting those objectives? What else? What help do you need?

Framework for Forward Focused Project Reviews:

1. What successes have we had since our last project review?

2. What specifically caused those successes? What can we learn from them?

3. What specific objectives are each of us working on right now?

4. What are the benefits to the overall project by accomplishing those? What are the benefits to your team? What will it do for you personally?

5. What specific actions can you take now to move closer to your objectives? Who will be responsible for those actions, and when will you complete them?

Framework for Problem Resolution:

1. Although we have this significant challenge, what are some things that are working, no matter how small? What else?

2. To what do we attribute those successes?

3. What is the specific goal we are trying to achieve in this situation?

4. What would be the benefits of accomplishing that objective (for all stakeholders)?

5. What could we do more, better or differently to move past this challenge and closer to our objective? Who will do what by when?

Framework for Developing Collaboration and Teamwork:

1. What are some things we are doing well as we work together as a team? What else? What are some things that worked well on other teams of which you have been a part?

2. What, specifically, caused each of those to work?

3. What is our vision of excellent collaboration and teamwork? What else?

4. What would be the benefits for each of the parties involved to accomplish that vision?

5. What can we do to move closer to that vision? What are each of us willing and committed to contribute?

Framework for Effective Project Startup:

1. What have you done successfully in similar projects?

2. What did you do as a project team that made it successful? What else?

3. What is your vision of how we want to work together on this project?

4. What are the benefits of doing so? For your clients, stakeholders, company, ourselves?

5. What are some things we could do:

    a. To move forward in those ways?

    b. To keep on track?

    c. To get back on track when we waver?

    d. What commitment will each project team member make toward contributing to this vision?

Framework for Effective Selling:

1. What do you like about your current service (product)? What else?

2. What is the specific advantage of each of those to you?

3. If you could describe the ideal service (product), what would it be? What else? How would (your differentiating feature) fit into your ideal?

4. What would be the benefits (to all stakeholders) to have the ideal service (product), or close to it? What would be the perceived value?

5. Step 5 in this case is not a question. Instead, it is your proposal for how you could support filling the gap between what they currently have and their ideal. If you cannot meet what they currently like and also fill the gap, or at least come close, you might not have a good solution.

About the Authors

Ed Oakley

After receiving a master's degree in engineering from Stanford University, Ed Oakley spent 15 years in the computer industry, mostly with Hewlett-Packard, managing as many as 300 people.

He has been on a continuing quest over the last 30 years to understand how to bring out the very best in people, teams and organizations.

Today, he is CEO of Enlightened Leadership Solutions, Inc., a multimillion dollar consulting and training firm focused on balancing the "hard" and "soft," the processes and people, to create measurable solutions by making leadership simple.

Ed is a well-known speaker, facilitator and consultant. He holds the National Speakers Association's Certified Speaking Professional award, and has been applauded by managers from over 65 countries.

Doug Krug

Doug is co-author with Ed of the best-selling book, *Enlightened Leadership: Getting to the HEART of Change.*

Doug is noted for helping top executive teams create and sustain the focus and alignment essential to successfully deal with today's most pressing leadership challenges. The essence of Doug's work is built around the premise that the core of what makes a leader cannot be taught – not in the traditional sense. It has to be brought out from within the individual.

Bring the *Leadership Made Simple* Message to Your Team in Five Additional Ways

Keynote Presentations
Kick off your next conference with an inspiring, dynamic presentation, customized with substance and value that gets to the heart of the matter most critical to you.

Onsite Leadership/Management Workshops & Seminars
We are passionate about helping you produce results quickly and more effectively by making leadership simple. Our workshops are guaranteed to get measurable results.

Leading Change Without Authority™
We specialize in developing and coaching professionals responsible for major initiatives across functional boundaries. They become outstanding leaders while experiencing action-learning that gets organizational results.

Train-the-Trainer Certification – Framework for Leadership™
Certify your in-house trainers and consultants to teach and use the Framework for Leadership as part of your management/leadership development programs and change initiatives.

Other Media:
- Audio learning series
- Video learning system
- Teleconference series

Contact Enlightened Leadership Solutions, Inc.
303.729.0540
www.enleadership.com

Accelerate Team Performance Package

The Next Level ... Leading Beyond the Status Quo provides insight and direction on what it takes to lead your team to a higher and greater Next Level. **$14.95**

Power Exchange – How to Boost Accountability & Performance in Today's Workforce This quick read offers practical strategies to help any leader boost accountability and performance in today's workforce. **$9.95**

Passionate Performance ... Engaging Minds and Hearts to Conquer the Competition offers practical strategies to engage the minds and heart of your team at home, work, church or community. Read it and conquer your competition! **$9.95**

I Quit, But Forgot to Tell You provides the straightforward, logical truths that lead to disengagement ... and provides the antidotes to prevent the virus from spreading within your organization. **$14.95**

Monday Morning Communications provides workable strategies to solving serious communications challenges. **$14.95**

180 Ways to Walk the Recognition Talk will help you provide recognition to your people more often and more effectively. **$9.95**

Lessons in Loyalty takes you inside Southwest Airlines to discover what makes it so different ... and successful. **$14.95**

The Manager's Coaching Handbook is a practical guide to improve performance from your superstars, middle stars and falling stars. **$9.95**

Start Right – Stay Right is every employee's straight talk guide to personal responsibility and job success. Perfect for every employee at every level. **$9.95**

Ouch! That Stereotype Hurts Regardless of your job title, you need to communicate with others to be successful. If you want to communicate respect through your message so that you can help build a workplace where all individuals feel included, this book is for you! **$12.95**

The Manager's Communication Handbook will allow you to connect with employees and create the understanding, support and acceptance critical to your success. **$9.95**

The CornerStone Perpetual Calendar, a compelling collection of quotes about leadership and life, is perfect for office desks, school and home countertops. **$14.95**

CornerStone Collection of Note Cards Sampler Pack is designed to make it easy for you to show appreciation for your team, clients and friends. The awesome photography and your personal message written inside will create a lasting impact. Pack of 12 (one each of all 12 designs) **$24.95**

Visit www.**CornerStoneLeadership**.com for additional books and resources.

☑ **YES! Please send me extra copies of** *Leadership Made Simple!*
1-30 copies $14.95   31-99 copies $13.95   100+ copies $12.95

Leadership Made Simple   —— copies X ——— = $ ———

Leadership Made Simple Companion Resources

PowerPoint® Presentation (downloadable)   —— copies X $99.95   = $ ———

Additional Team Performance Books

Accelerate Team Performance Package   —— pack(s) X $149.95 = $ ———
  (Includes one copy of *each* product listed
  on the previous page.)

Other Books

_____   —— copies X ——— = $ ———

_____   —— copies X ——— = $ ———

_____   —— copies X ——— = $ ———

Shipping & Handling $ ———
Subtotal $ ———
Sales Tax (8.25%-TX Only) $ ———
Total (U.S. Dollars Only) $ ———

Shipping and Handling Charges

Total $ Amount	Up to $49	$50-$99	$100-$249	$250-$1199	$1200-$2999	$3000+
Charge	$6	$9	$16	$30	$80	$125

Name _____ Job Title_____

Organization _____ Phone_____

Shipping Address _____ Fax_____

Billing Address_____E-mail _____
                                          (required when ordering PowerPoint® Presentation)
City_____ State _____ ZIP_____

❑ Please invoice (Orders over $200) Purchase Order Number (if applicable)_____

Charge Your Order: ❑ MasterCard   ❑ Visa   ❑ American Express

Credit Card Number _____ Exp. Date_____

Signature _____

❑ Check Enclosed (Payable to: CornerStone Leadership)

Fax	**Mail**	**Phone**
972.274.2884	P.O. Box 764087	888.789.5323
	Dallas, TX 75376	

www.**CornerStoneLeadership**.com

Thank you for reading *Leadership Made Simple.*
We hope it has assisted you in your quest for
personal and professional growth.

CornerStone Leadership is committed to provide new
and enlightening products to organizations worldwide.
Our mission is to fuel knowledge with practical resources
that will accelerate your team's productivity,
success and job satisfaction!

Best wishes for your continued success.

CornerStone
Leadership Institute
www.CornerStoneLeadership.com

*Start a crusade in your organization –
have the courage to learn, the vision to lead,
and the passion to share.*